Becoming a Pilgrim

Pilgrim, you that will leave for Compostelle, whatever your faith and your relation to God, know that He called you to this road, that He invited you to go all the way to the sanctuary of the apostle Jacques-le-Majeur. A pilgrimage is a personal act, but not an individual one. In this communion with believers, you walk on the footsteps of the believers and pilgrims of yesterday, and you precede those that will undertake this path tomorrow. Equip yourself as simply as possible and prepare yourself to live in sobriety.

Abandon the taste of the world for speed and the vanity of the feat. Take the time to listen, the time to look, the time to pray. If you want to be helped by God, don't count on yourself as much as on Him! Don't predict everything and prepare yourself to be guided by Him. Learn to meet the other as a brother who, in Christ's image, walks by your side and opens you their treasure. Discreet and respectful of the long and ancestral chain of pilgrims, know that the pilgrim is a free man in the sight and the tenderness of God: the spirit of confidence and of simplicity goes well beyond all the historic and traditional observances and conventions.

The "Creanciale" of the French Catholic Church

In the past, the pilgrim desiring to go to a distant sanctuary had to ask for a letter of recommendation from his Parish Priest. This letter testified to his state of being a pilgrim recommended to those that could offer him hospitality. It also served as a pass from the civil, military and ecclesiastic authorities met on the road.

Today, the "creanciale" is a sign of welcome from the Church toward future sincere pilgrims, making a deep, personal walk, and open to a spiritual path.

The "creanciale" is a document of recommendation that engages the one who delivers it like the one who, the length of the journey, presents it to their hosts, without asserting any right.

Even if the "creanciale" is not considered a legal administrative document, it represents a strong sign of belonging to the people of pilgrims and itinerants. Cleared of its usual, social, and professional attributes, the walker discovers on the road a simple identity of a pilgrim, of a searcher of God.

LETTERS
FROM THE WAY

A Walking Journey
Arles, France to Puente La Reina, Spain

BY BARBARA V. ANDERSON

LETTERS
FROM THE WAY

A Walking Journey

Arles, France to Puente La Reina, Spain

BY BARBARA V. ANDERSON

INCANTO PRESS
BURLINGAME, CALIFORNIA

Published in the United States by Incanto Press, Inc., Burlingame, California.

Library of Congress Control Number: 2014948355

Publisher's Cataloging-in-Publication data

Anderson, Barbara V.

    Letters from the way : a walking journey , Arles , France to Puenta La Reina, Spain / Barbara V. Anderson.

    p. cm.

    ISBN 978-1-941217-05-4

1. Anderson, Barbara V. --Travel --Spain, Northern. 2. Anderson, Barbara V. --Travel --France. 3. Christian pilgrims and pilgrimages --Travel --Spain--Santiago de Compostela . 4. Santiago de Compostela (Spain) --Description and travel. 5. Camino de Santiago de Compostela. I. Title.

BX2321.S3 A5 2014

263/.0424611 --dc23

Cover Illustration Copyright © 2014 by Incanto Press
Book Design and Production by Kate Davidson
Photo Editing by Irina Yuzhakova
Author Photograph by Steve Haag
Edited by Joanne Naiman

Printed in the United States of America

1 2 3 4 5 6 7 8 9

Carte Chemin d'Arles, page 1 © Carte extraite de l'ouvrage Le Chemin d'Arles, vers Saint-Jacques-de-Compostelle, éditions Rando Editions. Used with permission.

Cafe Terrace at Night, page 15, Vincent Willem van Gogh, Photo courtesy of Wikimedia Commons

Adam and Eve, page 44, Masolino da Panicale, Photo courtesy of Wikimedia Commons

Photo Contributors

Marie-Claude, cover, 21, 23 (lower left), 38

Peter Van Vilet, 54

Alberto Cabrera Agular, cover, 59, 60, 63

Maite Ozkoidi, 65 (top)

Michael Yamaguchi, 71 (top)

Barbara V. Anderson, 6, 9, 11, 15 – 20, 22, 23 (upper left, upper right, lower right), 25 – 28, 31 – 35, 37, 38, 41, 43, 45, 46, 49, 51, 52, 56, 59, 63, 65 (lower), 66, 70, 71

For the friends and family who read my weekly letters and encouraged me throughout my journey.

Contents

INTRODUCTION

In April 2012, I decided to take a walk, a very long walk. I walked 500 miles on the GR 65 in France from Le Puy-en-Velay to St-Jean-Pied-de-Port. In Spring 2013, I took another walk. I walked 600 miles on the GR 653, from Arles, France to Puente la Reina, Spain.

I didn't know much about long distance walking before I began my first trek. Raised Catholic (pre- and post- Vatican II), I knew about the *Camino de Santiago*. Pilgrims have walked this old trade route across Spain for over 1000 years and I probably would have walked it too but my timing was off. Just as I began making plans, Emilio Estevez released the film, *The Way*, starring his father, Martin Sheen. Martin walked the most popular Spanish route known as the *Camino Francés* (yes it is confusing, the most popular route in Spain is known as the French Road). It seemed everyone who saw the film decided to walk the *Camino de Santiago* from St Jean Pied au Port to Santiago de Compostela.

I wanted a quiet, contemplative walk and suddenly the *Camino de Santiago* was anything but quiet. That's when I discovered pilgrim trails throughout Europe, trails leading to the main Spanish trail. Traditionally, pilgrims began their journey from their homes—whether those homes were Germany, England, or Norway.

The Way of St.-James, St.-James's Way, St.-James's Path, or St.-James's Trail (commonly known by its name in Spanish: *El Camino de Santiago*) is the name of any of the pilgrimage routes (most commonly the *Camino Francés* or French route) to the shrine of the apostle St.-James the Great in the Cathedral of Santiago de Compostela in Galicia in northwestern Spain, where tradition has it that the remains of the saint are buried.

Four of these pilgrim trails, the *Chemins de St.-Jacques*, are in France and lead to the *Camino de Santiago*. France has hundreds of kilometers of secular trails called *Grandes Randonnées* (GRs). All four pilgrim trails are also part of the French trail system of *Grandes Randonnées*. The GR 65 and the GR 653 are two of these trails.

Most *Grandes Randonnées* offer *gîtes* (shared sleeping accommodations similar to hostels) along the route. I sent away for a guidebook to the *gîtes*, *Miam Miam Dodo,* (Vieux Crayon, 2013), which I took to the local French restaurant for help translating.

I never considered walking America's classic long distance trails, the Pacific Crest Trail or the Appalachian Trail. These trails require tent camping and hauling food and stoves. I may like walking alone, but I don't like camping alone. Perhaps one day I will get over that, but right now it is a bit too much *alone* for me.

I traveled solo on both adventures. There were no tours involved or even deep knowledge about what I should expect. I had no particular French language skills. What I wanted was, quite simply, a long walk.

You might ask, "Barbara, why on earth did you think it was a good idea to walk for 600 miles?" That would be a fair question but I would have to answer: why not? I am a walker and a walker walks. A walker walks when they are happy, when they are sad, when they are bored, when they are busy. A walker walks because there is nothing that offers more pleasure, sweeps away the cobwebs, frees the soul, grounds the body, or relaxes the mind. A walker walks to resolve problems, to forget problems, to understand problems. A walker walks for no reason and for every reason.

Walking is the sheer pleasure of putting one foot in front of the other, the journey along the trail. It is not about the arriving, it is about the doing. I'm a great fan of the purposeless walk—a walk for no reason other than the pleasure of the walk. Others prefer walks to some place—the bank, the post office, or the grocery store. Obviously, long walks are about getting somewhere, but for me the destination is just the excuse—the walk is about the walking. Even when the wind is blowing, the sky is hailing, and the trail seems impossibly uphill, there is nowhere else I would rather be.

The walk was not to prove anything, to lose weight, or to get in shape. The walk was not a life-long dream or an entry on a bucket list. In fact, I don't believe in bucket lists, at least not bucket lists that are somebody else's list of things you should do before you die. Those lists are about the end, not about the doing. They're about ticking off where you got to, not about the getting there. No, the walk was definitely not a checkmark on a bucket list.

A friend asked, "What on earth do you think about?" Well, if I were Benjamin Franklin,

Ludwig van Beethoven, Gustav Mahler, Erik Satie, Pyotr Tchaikovsky, Søren Kierkegaard, Immanuel Kant, Ludwig Wittgenstein, or any of the other great walkers, I might have truly great thoughts. But I'm not them, so here is what I think about.

Some days I think about blue skies, billowing clouds, rainbows, bird songs, soft breezes, colorful flowers, undulating hills, shifting shadows, dappled leaf patterns, Technicolor butterflies, cowbells, meandering sheep and cuckoo songs. Some days I am completely content.

Some days I think my pack is too heavy, my foot hurts, I'm thirsty, tired, too hot, too cold. I wonder how far I have walked and if this trail can continue uphill forever. Can I make it to the next town before I need a toilet? Some days I think this will never end.

Some days I think about how to solve a problem, what a character should say, or what I should do. I write scripts and stories, create lists, make decisions. Some days everything becomes clear.

Some days I think what I should have said, what I could have done, what I would have done if only—but now it's too late. He died before I could say goodbye. Did I do enough? I never said, I would have said, I should have said. I should have been there. Some days I cry.

Some days I think nothing, nothing at all.

Some days I think all of these things and more.

There was another reason I thought the *Camino de Santiago* was not right for me. I knew true believers cross Spain walking under the Milky Way, but I am not a true believer. Or a true atheist. I am not any kind of believer. It made sense to me to walk a path that leads to The Path. Was I expecting to find God? I don't know. If there is a God, perhaps he could find me. Like walking with the Sierra Singles, you're not really looking, but possibly you'll be found.

The letters are my reflections along the way. They are my musings about the weather and my fellow pilgrims, about vultures and butterflies, about lessons to learn and spiritual questions to answer. They are not a travelogue, a daily blog of events, or recommendations for the best places to stay. They are, however, a good resource if you are wondering what it would be like to set out on your own and take a long, a very long walk.

At the beginning of my walk I wrote only to family and a few close friends but by the end I was writing to more than 50 friends. I left these letters largely unchanged to preserve all that I did not know about the coming rains or the personalities of the people I would meet.

I hope you enjoy my journey and in reading the letters it becomes your journey too.

Spring 2012

Prologue

Prologue

Last Year's Journey

In mid-May, 2012, I leave for France to walk the GR 65. I cash in miles to fly to Paris and buy a ticket for the train, or rather a series of trains, to Le Puy-en-Velay.

The last train is only one car with a driver's seat at both ends. The woman across from me has short hair dyed reddish-brown and one of those faces that smile even when the corners of her mouth don't lift. Her name is Ode Pactat-Didier and she is the author of many books about the *Chemin*. She informs me that my route was originally walked not by Catholic pilgrims, but by alchemists from ancient times, that the churches of Le Puy-en-Velay were built on prehistoric altars, and that I will meet Isis. Isis, really?

When the train curves around a mountain, a jumble of stone houses and tile roofs comes into view. We arrive to Le Puy-en-Velay—equally famous for churches and lentils. Three spires rise above this red and grey mosaic. On the highest hill is a red cast-iron statue of Mary cradling baby Jesus. Jesus' right arm is outstretched as if waving. Close to the statue is the massive Cathédrale Notre-Dame du Puy. On a third precipice is the small Chapelle Saint-Michel d'Aiguilhe, perched precariously high in the air, like an upside down ice cream cone.

I retrieve my iPad. Yes, I have my iPad. If I am going to find God I need information. I need Wikipedia. I need Google. I am not just an American walking the *Chemin*, I am doing what I know how to do. I am Googling for God.

Google informs me that in ancient times men climbed this volcanic chimney to worship the Dolmen. (A Dolmen is a stone tomb dating from 4000 BC.) The Romans converted this Dolmen into an altar to Mercury; the messenger who wore winged sandals. That seems appropriate for a long walk. The Christians converted the Dolmen into a chapel dedicated to St Michael, the patron saint of high places. Think metaphysical recycling.

Early the next morning, I head to the Cathedral for the pilgrim mass. After the mass the priest gathers the pilgrims together to bless us and send us on our way. Many have already walked hundreds of miles—from Poland, Amsterdam, Italy—in order to arrive to Le Puy-en-Velay to walk the *Chemin de St.-Jacques* to the *Camino de Santiago* where they will walk on to *Santiago de Compestela*. We are each asked to carry a folded slip of paper on which others have written a prayer. I tuck a yellow slip of paper into my coat pocket without looking at it.

In the gift shop, I register for my *créanciale*. The *créanciale* is a passport that qualifies me as a pilgrim and permits me to sleep in *gîtes*. When I begin my journey, it means no more to me than a license to get me what I want—cheap lodging. Every *gîte* stamps my passport with a unique symbol showing where I have been and blank spaces for where I am going. By the time I finish my trek, the *créanciale* is my most valued possession.

The church has a massive souvenir shop. I buy a map and a scallop shell—nothing more. When carrying everything on my back I quickly learn to carry nothing more than what I need and I need very little. But this gift shop is a shopper's paradise, as if the money exchanged for the various sizes of plastic statues of St.-Jacques and straw hats replicating his famous chapeau have replaced traditional alms.

The cathedral is grand with multi-colored stones, ornate carvings, six large cupolas, gilded wood and pretty much every architectural style of the last 1000 years. And the cathedral has its own set of myths and miracles.

In the first century AD, a woman suffering from a fever was inspired to visit the Dolmen—yes, another prehistoric Dolmen. She fell into a feverish sleep. When she awoke, the Virgin Mary was seated next to her. Mary cured her fever and told her to build a cathedral. The cathedral was built over the Dolmen and Catholics continued to believe in its healing powers. Pilgrims came to the church to stretch out on the stone and wait for their cure.

In the center of the altar is not the expected crucifix with the dying Christ. No, in the center of this altar is a small, very small, doll. It is a statue of a black Mary holding Jesus. She is wearing . . . how should I put this . . . she is wearing a pyramid, a quilted white pyramid festooned with little bows and covering all but her face. A hole in the center reveals that the face of Jesus is also black.

This is not the original. The original was a pagan Earth Mother. The first Christians came here to sleep on a prehistoric Dolmen and worship a doll. We never covered this in Catechism class.

A Moorish artist carved the second from cedar. Even though she looks like the Egyptian goddess Isis (just as Ode foretold) holding her immaculately conceived child Horus, the Church calls her Mary holding her immaculately conceived child Jesus. There is a saying amongst actors, good actors borrow and great actors steal. The Catholic Church may be a great actor.

The third, a resin replica, was created after French Revolutionaries destroyed most Black Madonnas with cries of death to the Egyptian goddess.

Pale-skinned Mary symbolizes obedience and purity whereas the Black Madonna (*La Vierge Noire*) represents female sexuality, Diana, Artemis, Venus, Aphrodite. Catholicism, home of the feminine mystic? Well ruby-red hiking boots, we're clearly not in the Baltimore Catechism any more.

In my first *gîte* I sleep in a room with fourteen others. Unbeknownst to me, these people will become my new best friends and for the next few weeks we will walk, sleep, eat, and possibly save

each other's lives—Carmen and Denis from Montreal, four walking buddies from Marseilles, and three couples from the Paris suburbs. I have not yet learned their importance.

Gîtes are where pilgrims sleep and I am a pilgrim. To be honest, *gîtes* are the scariest part of my trip. I am not "sort of" an introvert. I scored 27 out of 29 on a test for introverts. People exhaust me. Sleeping, eating, talking, sharing bath facilities with strangers is much scarier than walking 500 miles. Walking is simply putting one foot in front of the other and trying not to get too lost. A lot like life.

But people—people scare me. Being with people really scares me. Being with people all the time terrifies me.

What if the *gîtes* are full of boisterous extroverts? What if there are groups of people who ignore you and who talk and laugh late into the night? Even worse, what if they don't ignore you but want to make you talk and laugh late into the night?

Come to think of it, what if there is a heaven and heaven is full of extroverts? What if God is an extrovert—I mean if there is a God—he must be an extrovert. An introvert wouldn't need people and certainly wouldn't fill his own home with strangers.

Everything about this overpopulated, under-stimulated place called heaven horrifies me. Maybe I don't believe in God because I don't want to end up in heaven. People who have those near-death experiences always talk about being in a dark tunnel with this beam of light with all your relatives waiting at the other end. Eternity with all my relatives—hmm.

The next morning, I am the first awake. I am still on California time. On the counter, the proprietor sets out the coffee, hot milk, bread, butter, and jam known as a French breakfast. I do what I think any American would do. I pour myself a bowl of coffee and hot milk, sit down at the table, and start sipping. A few minutes later the next person awake takes the plates and bowls from the counter and sets the table. Soon, several people are working together to put out the coffee and bread for everyone to breakfast together. Only one person, the lone American, me, is sitting at the table already sipping.

Along the way I meet dozens of interesting people, many of whom are women. It is my impression that there are wives and mothers all over France who one morning over breakfast, simply walk to the door and as they open it, they look back and say, "Goodbye dears, I am going for a walk." And they leave for a week or more.

Every day is the same. We breakfast, walk, shower, wash clothes, dine, and sleep. It is a rhythm that is every day the same and every day extraordinarily unique. One day we walk over Mt Aubrac, a 1300-meter rise. The wind blows straight at us, 110 km per hour. The trail is hidden under the snow and ice. I am walking with four of my new best friends, the walking buddies from Marseilles. We huddle into a human version of *March of the Penguins*. When we arrive at the summit, we drink a toast to Mt Aubrac and our safe arrival. Later we learn how lucky we have been as three others will perish from exertion during the next ten days.

Approaching the beautiful village of Conques, I hear American voices—an unusual sound on this trail. The couple introduces themselves and hands me a business card advertising their blog. If they had handed me a bolt of lightning I could not have had more of a shock. The truth is, I thought about blogging and business cards. They are Californians and we Californians understand the importance of maintaining our connections. We keep the world abreast of our every thought.

As a writer, I often look at my life as something to tell to others. After all, that is what I am doing now. But it is different if in the moment, in every moment, we are compelled to tell our friends everything. "Here look, here are the people I am with. Here is a photo of me posing where I am. Here, this is what I am looking at, well maybe not looking at because I am busy showing it to you, I can look at it later when I have time."

I disconnect, well almost. Once a week I send a letter to my family and friends. But I disconnect from the immediacy of posting to the stratosphere known as the Net. My thoughts are no longer thought for the entertainment of others. This is a big step for a writer to take.

I walk and walk and walk. Five hundred miles later and 60 km before my destination, I develop severe tendinitis in my right foot. The *gîte* proprietress sees my limp, insists I go to with her to the pharmacy and within ten minutes the entire village crowds into the pharmacy to give their opinions on whether I can finish my *Chemin*. The village vote is "No, you must stop".

I negotiate. Finally, after being massaged, medicated and bandaged, I promise the village (yes it takes a village) I will send my backpack ahead, I will stop to rest if the swelling gets worse, and when I arrive in St Jean Pied au Port I will finish altogether. I will not continue into Spain. I obtain the village's permission to continue.

When I arrive in Saint-Jean-Pied-de-Port on the border of Spain, all my new friends are going on to Santiago. I want to continue too, but I don't. I promised the village I would stop. I stop. I stop knowing I will be back. I will walk in France and Spain and who knows where else. I have discovered the joy of long distance walking and this is just the beginning not the end.

Oh, the slip of yellow paper in my pocket said: "I pray for Gabrielle. Please make our love grow and become stronger. With love, R." Good luck R. I hope your prayer comes true.

Spring 2013

The Letters

LETTER ONE
Before Beginning
Arles
May 13 – 17

I arrived in Arles on May 13 after a long trip on multiple planes and trains. I am staying four nights to acclimatize myself to the nine-hour time shift and enjoy the city. This is a small town with a big history, from the Roman bath and amphitheater, the Spanish bullfight ring and school, and Van Gogh's most famous paintings including *Café Terrace, Place du Forum*. The actual café is painted (for the tourists) to look as much like Van Gogh's painting as possible. I suppose this is one version of life imitating art.

Today I took the city bus, which turned out to be the school bus, from Arles to the Pont de Gau Ornithological Park in the Camargue. The Camargue has red rice, grey salt, black bulls, white horses and pink flamingoes. I spent most of the day walking through the reed ponds and marshes of the park. I never saw a flock of flamingoes before (not counting drunken student pranks and a lawn full of plastic pink creatures). A flock of flying flamingoes is a cloud of pink feathers tinged with the blackest of black at the wingtips. Their necks do not stretch out the way

Cafe Terrace at Night (1888)
Vincent Willem van Gogh
(Photo courtesy of *Wikimedia Commons*)

The Camargue horse is an ancient breed of horse indigenous to the Camargue. It is considered one of the oldest breeds of horses in the world. For centuries, these small horses have lived wild in the harsh environment of the Camargue marshes and wetlands where they developed the stamina, hardiness and agility for which they are known today.

of most other birds but rather form a sinewy curve with a touch more black at the beak.

Actually there are 400 species of birds including herons, egrets, swans, eagles, hawks, and harriers. (I didn't actually count so I am believing the brochure which also says there are 10,000 flamingoes—I didn't count those either.) Being spring, all were either nesting or swimming about with newly minted families.

In the evening I walked a few more kilometers to Saintes-Maries-de-la-Mer. The town is chock-a-block with the caravans of *gitans* (gypsies) arriving from all over Europe. This weekend begins the *Procession de Sainte-Sara* (Saint Sara looks suspiciously like the Black Madonna reminiscent of the beginning of last year's walk from Le Puy-en-Velay).

When the city/school bus arrives, I attempt to buy a ticket back to Arles. Despite my beginner French classes, I cannot say the word "Arles" to any Frenchman and be understood. As far as I can tell, it is pronounced by swallowing one's own tongue, a talent I have yet to master. A schoolchild, whose command of English is far better than my French, rescues me.

Tomorrow my walk starts in earnest. It has rained heavily every day and of course everyone says it never rains this time of year and how unusual and yada-yada-yada . . . anyway it is wet, very, very wet. Hopefully the rains will not last much longer.

Sent Friday evening, May 17

Best wishes to all, Barbara

LETTER TWO
Starting Out
Arles to St-Guilhem-Le-Désert
May 22

This walk is much more difficult than last year's. There are fewer hikers and the trail is not well marked. The first day I set out from Arles walking alone following my landlady's hand-drawn map. I had expected to buy a trail map in Arles but they were sold out. Within a few kilometers from town, I took a wrong turn and for the first time in my hiking career, I tumbled head over heels down a hill. I lay there thinking, "I'm dead on the first day of my trip." Then I looked around and realized, "Oh God, I'm lying in a garbage dump." I decided I could do better than to die in a garbage dump in France. That night at the *gîte* in Saint-Gilles, a Norwegian man said he fell in the snow coming into Arles and decided the same—there was no way a Norwegian could die in French snow.

The next day was unbelievably rainy and windy with lightning and thunder. I walked with four men from Orleans and Alfred from Switzerland. We were all thoroughly exhausted. I think the beautiful white horses on the green fields of the Camargue were a sight to behold but honestly I just wanted the day to end.

The way to Montpellier was easy and the weather perfect. I stayed an extra day and fell in love with the city. It is a university town, in fact, one of the oldest universities in the world. This is a holiday weekend—Pentecost Sunday and Monday, so most tourist attractions and churches are closed. What a perfect excuse to wander aimlessly and people-watch at cafés.

French students are fashionable even when dressed casually, but I don't understand how they keep those lovely scarves so perfectly draped. I admit that I have a suspicion that the deep dark secret of the French is they dispose of any children who are not absolutely adorable. And honestly, I am mystified by people who have all day to sit in outdoor cafes, but no time to pick up the droppings of their petits chiens. And what the heck is Pentecost Monday if all the churches are locked? Also, my gaydar is broken here as all French men (please do not quote me) dress "gay" (at least that is my impression). It's charming but confusing to a woman from San Francisco where for many straight men dressing up means putting on a clean T-shirt with a logo from their latest start-up.

The next day I began early with a 30 km hike in mind but somehow I turned off the trail. Finally, I found the trail again and arrived at a road where I met another hiker. Marie-Claude asked my destination. I explained I was walking toward Saint-Guilhem-le-Désert. She explained I was walking in the opposite direction; I was walking toward Montpellier. I explained I had just come from Montpellier and that she must be turned around. She explained that it was I who was turned around. I insisted I was right. She insisted she was right. Finally she convinced me by walking to a trail marker pointing the way to Saint-Guilhem-le-Désert. So, four hours and 16 km later, after circling and circling, I found myself back where I began. I joined Marie-Claude walking—finally—in the correct direction. I have great confidence in friendships that begin with a quarrel and end in a smile.

Marie-Claude is from Montpellier and speaks no English. Hopefully my French will improve (though I still cannot say 'Arles'). She is about my age and wears a constant smile. She has taken time off from being a wife, mother and grandmother to walk from Montpellier to Castres. Since we are walking the same route, we have decided to walk together. I changed my reservations to match hers. I will be exactly one day behind the schedule I sent to all of you before I left California.

Marie-Claude

We are now in the picturesque touristic village of Saint-Guilhem-le-Désert. While Marie-Claude hikes to the tiny chapel at the top of the mountain, I wander along snaking cobblestones. Ancient stone buildings creep up a green hillside with endless views of the Gellone Valley. The town and abbey came into existence as a medieval staging post for pilgrims, but today it is mostly upscale *auberges* and restaurants. If much of the monastery looks familiar it is because this is the church used to create the New York Metropolitan Cloisters.

All sorts of women on vacation are wearing tight dresses, leather jackets and stilettos. I am wearing two layers of merino wool, a purple raincoat and hiking boots and am reminded of just what a slog this can be. There is a point where a brush through one's hair and another brush of the teeth seems like all the effort one can exert.

We are not sleeping in one of the fancy *auberges* but rather in the most rustic of rustic *gîtes*. *Gîtes*—what an amazing system, especially for women. Every trail has any number of private

and municipal *gîtes* located between 20 and 35 km apart. You can reserve a bed and usually the *demi-pension*—breakfast, dinner and a bed. When *demi-pension* is not offered, there is a fully equipped kitchen (*coin cuisine*). *Gîtes* are especially a boon for women who can walk alone or with one or two friends knowing they will have a bed, dinner and breakfast, a hot shower and companions with whom to chat. Accommodations vary from private homes to attractive B&Bs with private or semi-private rooms, to dormitory style rooms, to basic barracks. Yes, the bed might be the top or bottom of a bunk and men and women sleep in the same room but for 9 to 15 euro a night or 20 to 35 with *demi-pension*, it is still quite a bargain. And it is energizing to meet so many women (married or single) who just felt like taking a long walk.

With so many interesting women, there are of course the *loups du Chemin*. These usually are the German or Swiss German men (the cultural reasons for this elude me) who walk the *Chemin* every year looking for women. Some are blatant, others more devious, but annoying all the same. Last year there was the retired (and married) atomic energy executive who casually asked between the salad course and the duck *confit*, "if you are walking for eight weeks, what are you doing for sex?" And then he offered his services. Then there was Michael from Bavaria who has spent the past dozen years having a yearly "romance" and a new winter vacation location.

On the second day of this trip, I walked 35 km in the wind and rain—a big mistake—too far too fast for the first days. One of the men I walked with was Alfred from Switzerland. That night I spent vomiting and with the shakes from sheer exhaustion. Alfred kept coming into my room with a bottle of rosé trying to get me to drink with him. As best I could figure out, he was trying to get me drunk and weak-willed between fits of retching. Really, Alfred? Sex between fits of vomiting? Really?

And while I am on the topic of trail pests, I may as well mention the *punaises de lit*, bed bugs. France is on a crusade against these creatures, but the odd thing is it may be the *gîtes* that are winning. A pilgrim may only bring their sleeping clothes, sleep sack, toiletries and valuables into the sleeping room—their pack stays in the foyer in a large green plastic trash bag. In the morning the sleep sack and clothes are sprayed, put into a sealed plastic sack and packed away for the next location. The nicer hotels and *auberges* can hardly ask their guests to leave their luggage in the hallway, so they are actually more susceptible. Pay more, get more

Written Wednesday evening, May 22

Not sure when I will actually send this mail—maybe soon maybe later.

I hope all are well—
Tomorrow we are heading straight up hill.
Barbara

LETTER THREE

Hilltops
Saint-Guilhem-Le-Désert To Lodève
May 24

Leaving Saint-Guilhem-le-Désert was like hiking part way up the switchbacks of the Grand Canyon and then coming back down and hiking up twice more. It was worth the trip though—exquisitely beautiful views of the deep gorge we are circumventing.

It is similar to Northern California but as a result of all the rain, everything is lush and green. Marie-Claude says they have never seen anything like it, as normally it should indeed be dryer, well, it should be more like Northern California.

Tonight we are in Lodève. There is an amazing cathedral across the road from our *gîte* and interestingly, and a bit oddly, a mosque next door. We were shown to our *gîte* by a group of very considerate Muslim men who were arriving at their mosque for Friday prayers. To add to the idiosyncratic nature of the place, Marie-Claude and I bought our supper on a street selling only Polish foods and decorations. Quite a lot of diversity packed into a small village! The gothic cathedral is simply beautiful with a polygonal apse lit by nine twelve-meter high stained glass windows (by Alexander Mauvernay)—yes, that's 9 windows each 36 feet tall! I have a lot of issues with Catholicism but they can sure build some glorious churches.

I know some of you are using Google Maps to track my adventure. Don't. The GR 653 is purposely laid out to take in every mountain-view and small village—so yes, it is about the journey not the destination. What looks like 30 km on Google Maps is probably more like 60 km with several hilltops thrown in—In other words why go around it when you can go over it or through it.

And to answer the question posed in a few of your emails, yes it is worth it. There is nothing like the slow walk approaching a village, the sheer joy of a hot shower at the end of the journey, dinner with the other pilgrims, eating local cheeses never sold on commercial markets, and ok, buying really good wine for one euro 56 cents.

This is Friday night May 24.

Tomorrow is a huge day—I think a 1000-meter climb so I best get some sleep. My best to everyone. Let me know what you are all up to.

I hear thunder. Yikes, oh yikes!
Barbara

LETTER FOUR

Mistral Noir
Lodève to Joncels
May 25

The walk from Lodève to Joncels was my introduction to the concept of being "blown off the mountain." A cold wet wind blew rain and hail so ferociously that we had to zigzag our way up the mountain leaning into the wind like arctic penguins. It was the famous *mistral* winds I had always associated with clear skies, impressionist artists, and romantic songs but this was the *mistral noir* associated with tragically fast winds, rain and snow, and I suspect very little in the way of songs or romance.

The weather cleared for the trip down the hill bringing sunshine, yellow and lavender flowers, green rolling hills, and endless vistas. If I had been able to speak English to Marie-Claude, the words I would have used to describe the afternoon would have been "verdant, luxuriant, bucolic, serene, undulating, lush". The words I would have used to describe the morning in the wind would have been "get me the f. . . off this mountain".

As some of you know walking the *Chemin* has a lot to do with my quest to discover God—figuring if I go where (s)he is supposed to hang out—well maybe, just maybe. All I can say is (s)he sure is making it difficult!

I have gotten a better understanding of the difference between the pilgrim route and the road—a recent day was a 33 km walk, but it would have been 20 km by road—and yes, especially on wet days, some pilgrims opt for walking on the road instead of the *Chemin*. This brings up the whole question "what is a pilgrim?" Everyone has his or her own definition. There are those who carry everything and only sleep in tents. There are those, like me, who carry everything, walk the actual *Chemin* and sleep in *gîtes*. There are those who have everything delivered by taxi between destinations and only carry a daypack and often sleep in the nicer private *auberges* or hotels. There are those who only walk when they feel like it and have themselves delivered by taxi. Everyone is a bit judgmental about what constitutes a pilgrim. Many of the municipal and some of the private *gîtes* do require that you walk or bike and a few require you to carry your own pack. I heard about a mother and her two daughters who drove between destinations and then slung on their packs just before villages to walk in and claim their place in the *gîtes*. I guess she wanted to teach her daughters her family values.

We are now in Joncels at the loveliest of lovely *gîtes*. The 80-year old father of the proprietor creates wonderful and whimsical animals from gnarled tree limbs and these decorate every inch of wall space and hang from the ceiling as mobiles.

Several different hiking trails (GRs) converge in Joncels so we have met many weekend hikers. While the others are at Saturday evening mass, I am nursing a Campari in front of a fire where a dozen wet hiking boots, including mine, are stuffed with newspaper (I suppose theirs were all supposed to be waterproof too) hopefully drying for tomorrow's assault on the mountain. I am wearing the heavy fleece jacket of the proprietress as I am carrying only lightweight clothes, a swimsuit and large tube of sun block for the normal weather of a Mediterranean May. It is always a punishment to pack incorrectly for a trip—it is hell to lug your useless possessions up and down mountains on your back.

We gather slowly for the group dinner—I think all are unusually hungry after the day fighting the wind and cold. Speaking of food, maybe I will explain a bit more about eating in a *gîte*. *Demi-pension* is breakfast and dinner. Breakfast is coffee and milk and bread, butter, and preserves. Cornflakes and Coco puffs are often available but no bowls as here these cereals are eaten dry. If the host is used to foreigners there may be fresh fruit and yogurt but that is an unusual treat. Every once in a while there is a hard-boiled egg but if a French person takes an egg, they are only saving it for lunch. I tried to explain to one *gîte* operator that I didn't eat bread preferring yogurt or just coffee. She very kindly made us crêpes, which obviously missed the point.

Dinner is almost always four—mayb—five courses. Some *gîtes* offer an appetizer course of ham, sausage or pâtés and an appetizer wine. This was more common on the Le Puy route. Next a homemade soup or a salad and of course, red wine. We've been getting a lot of tasty soups in an attempt to warm us up. Then comes the main course. On the Le Puy route dinner was always duck, sausage or duck sausage. French sausage has as little in common with our American basil/turkey offerings as cheap liverwursts with a good pâté. Let's face it, there are just times when pork fat tastes good. The most memorable meal last year was in the Aubrac, famous for *aligot*—mashed potatoes, cheese, and *crème fraîche* cooked in a huge pan and stirred with a wooden paddle by a strong man and served with more of those tasty French sausages.

This year's route features pork or sausage with a potato dish, beef bourguignon, or a complex couscous. Well, except for the bad *gîtes* (two so far) that insult us with chicken and rice. One *gîte* gave me a huge plate of plain rice and a rather small chicken leg. I was tempted to complain until I saw that the man sitting next to me had been given only the chicken back with his rice. Fortunately these meals are the exception not the rule. Often an immense cheese board of local specialties is offered before the dessert of a tart or *crème brûlée*.

Dinner is served restaurant style, or brought to you in your own kitchen and left with you to set your table and wash your dishes, or best of all, served family style with the host sitting down with you and sharing your meal. Dinner almost always starts at 7 or 7:30 and lasts 2 hours. Given that we are all of us in bed by 9:30, you can pretty much see how the evening evolves.

Sent Saturday May 25

Well I love you all but it is time to eat.
Stay dry,
Barbara

LETTER FIVE

Clear Skies
Joncels to Murat-Sur-Vèbre
May 27

Lovely day, lovely weather over mountaintops of the Parc Naturel Régional (upper Languedoc)—views to end all views of lakes and oak forests and finally a rocky descent over granite blocks into Saint-Gervais-sur-Mare. This was the weather we should be having every day but will only have for two days before the rains begin again.

France has more forest land than anywhere else in Europe and for two days we have had the joy of walking up and over forested mountains, yellow broom surrounded by purple and white flowers, waterfalls and rushing rivers, deciduous beech trees just budding, and evergreens bursting with new growth. One day there were fields and fields of Johnny Jump-Up Violas, a flower that I plant every spring in my garden. Its yellow and blue face holds so much history for me that it makes me both happy and sad to walk through this profusion of memories.

We have walked away from the weather of the Mediterranean and into the weather of the Atlantic. That should mean a change in the weather but to be honest, the forecast looks pretty much the same. Starting tomorrow it is supposed to rain every day. Sigh.

Sent Monday May 27

C'est la vie!
Moi

LETTER SIX
Gendarmerie *and the* Chemin
Murat-Sur-Vèbre to Castres
June 1

Gendarmerie and *Chemin*—it eventually had to happen. Thursday night the youngest of the pilgrims, a French girl in her gap year between high school and college, got lost, tearfully, painfully lost. At about 5:00 PM, when a dozen or so pilgrims were in the kitchen planning our evening meal and drying out our wet clothes, Elise telephoned the *gîte*. Marie-Claude and the others brought out maps, relayed instructions, and called in the *gendarmerie*. Finally by 8:30, she was found by a cow herder and safely driven to the *gîte*. She was in the middle of a forest, in pouring rain, wet and cold, and rightfully very afraid.

It had been an easy day to get lost. The rain came down nonstop. Clouds combined with fog making visibility almost impossible. The trails were all forest tracks with no breaks for houses, villages or roads. Marie-Claude and I have been lost at some point at least four out of the past five days. Why? First I must explain what we are following to find our way along the *Chemin*. The *Chemin* is one of France's *Grandes Randonnées* (GR). All the GRs (the secular routes as well as the Pilgrim routes) are marked with four signs each about three inches wide and three inches high. A single white line painted on top of a single red line means you are on the right road. An "×" of a red line over a white line means this is the wrong path (ah, if life could only be so simple). A white tail on the left side of three horizontal lines means turn right. A white tail on the right side means turn left. The markings can be painted on trees, houses, the backs of stop signs, bridge railings, stone walls, railroad crossings, rocks, lamp, and fence posts. They can be on either side of the road and there is no prescribed distance between markings. You may walk five or more kilometers on a road without any markings and it is the correct *Chemin* or you may see a marking every few meters. Sometimes all the markings are negative and you walk down the only road that does not have an "×" even though that road does not have a go ahead sign either. It is a sort of life or death version of "Where's Waldo?"

You only know you have walked on the wrong road when you arrive at a crossroads and there is no indication of where to go next. Furthermore, the route is marked identically in both directions. If you get turned around you will, as I did on the day I first met Marie-Claude, walk back to where you began. Every GR is marked identically so if one GR crosses another GR you must be careful to stay on your own route. Every GR has variants, which take you on slightly different walks to the same place or take you days out of your way. You may never know you are on a variant until you end up in a village tens of kilometers away from where you thought you were heading. You may, if you wish, take all of this as a metaphor for life including the part about getting lost.

But all of this was true last year so why is this year so different? For one thing there are just fewer people. About 3,000 people per year walk the Arles Route (this year) whereas every year 25,000 people walk the Le Puy route (last year). There are probably even fewer people on this route this year. Because of the terrible weather many pilgrims have dropped off, deciding to hitch a ride to the next big city and become tourists instead of pilgrims.

We lost our three Swiss friends when they made this decision. Sometimes the five of us walked together; sometimes we had reservations to sleep at the same *gîte*. The three met as part of a walking group but expanded their walks to include two weeks a year as pilgrims. I am sorry we did not have a chance to say goodbye and exchange emails. They were the only ones who walked without walking sticks and when the rains came, they walked with brightly colored umbrellas like three tropical flowers moving along the *Chemin*.

Sometimes our route markers have been removed. At the beginning of this route we crossed many vineyards, apple, and cherry orchards. Six of us came upon a cherry orchard with trees laden with ripe fruit. We couldn't resist, well more accurately, we didn't resist. And this lack of restraint by the pilgrims has caused some farmers to insist on rerouting the *Chemin*. Sometimes the farmers simply obliterate the *Chemin* markings. (I did not know we were forbidden to eat the fruit but had I known, it would have been all that much sweeter.) This problem did not exist last year because we mostly walked through duck farms and livestock and we pilgrims are urban enough that I doubt anyone catches a duck, wrings its neck, plucks it and cooks it. Cherries, grapes, and apples are of course another temptation altogether.

Another problem has been the unseasonably cold rain. Leaving La Salvetat-sur-Agout, Marie-Claude and I gingerly climbed down icy stone steps trying desperately not to slip. Ice, May, and Southern France are not words that belong in the same sentence. Tuesday through Friday the rain was torrential with hail, lightning, and thunder. This route weaves deep inside of forests with few if any crossings of civilization. Most of the time we were knee-deep in mud except when we were thigh-deep. Creeks have become rushing rivers, delightful to look at, but absolutely frightening to cross. The moss and lichen on the stones are beautifully dense but also treacherous and our eyes are constantly fixed on the path—consequently we have missed a few turns and had to backtrack when we realized we had gone astray. Marie-Claude and I have become philosophical about our daily "detours".

And finally there was Thursday, the day that Elise became so lost. Lumbermen were logging the forest and they cut down the trees marking the *Chemin* and covered our trail with branches and logs. We clamored over and through their leavings only guessing we were on the right path,

or for that matter, any path at all. I was the first to spot a tree with our beloved red and white marking and literally kissed it when we knew we were once again on the *Chemin* and heading toward our *gîte* and out of the rains.

There are other trail markings that differentiate the Pilgrim *Chemin*s from other GRs. These are the crosses—not many but some small metal or stone crosses where pilgrims stop to pray and leave one of the stones they are carrying—yes stones. Pilgrims carry them from home. Their friends sometimes give them stones to carry for them. I love you all and will carry your metaphysical stones if you like, but you have very little chance of convincing me to lug a kilo of stones around in my pack. Anyway, the metaphysical stones are heavy enough.

Tuesday night, our *gîte* was a tranquil log cabin on the lakefront with a big wood burning fire and picture windows from which to view the lake and the pouring rain. The other three pilgrims who were to share our home never turned up so we each had a private room with a double bed,

a roaring fire, and our *demi-pension* meal delivered to us with a bottle of good red wine. I began reading *The Burgess Boys* on my iPad. In the morning it was only Marie-Claude coming into my room, where I had a bowl of hot tea, my wonderful new book, propped up on pillows in the warmth of the *gîte* with the beautiful views, saying *"Barbara, prend courage, prend courage"* that finally got me motivated to walk again in the rain—or I would surely still be there now.

And what good fortune it turned out to be. The next night's stay was at the home of Robert Passeport. Many of the *gîtes* on this trail are simply rooms in private homes. Robert made us feel warm and comfortable as he hung our wet clothes high above a pot-bellied stove and created a masterful gourmet meal. Marie-Claude and I were Robert's only guests. After dinner I saw that Robert had a guitar. He said he only was learning to play and was actually a singer. He sang some French songs for us. He has a rich tenor voice. Afterward, he and I used my iPad to find lyrics to French and Italian songs—"Torna a Surriento", Edith Piaf, Jacques Brel, etc. We sang duets late into the night. Meeting someone whose voice matches your own, and singing those words from Piaf's "Non, Je Ne Regrette Rien", *"Car ma vie, car mes joies, Aujourd'hui, ça commence avec toi."*—is like a brief and stolen romance, a moment completely out of reality. Afterward Marie-Claude was sure to tell everyone that I could sing and I have been hit again and again with the command from other pilgrims, *"Chantez! Chantez!"*

And now I am in Castres for two days. Marie-Claude, who became such a great and patient companion, ended her walk. I owe so much to her for keeping me going when my determination waned. We had a farewell glass of champagne and I will truly miss her constant good cheer. When I begin again tomorrow, I will be on my own.

I have chosen for these two nights in Castres to stay alone in a hotel and recuperate—wash

clothes, repair my body, eat fresh fruits from the market in the plaza. My clothes were quite a problem. In general, the French do not use clothes dryers, depending instead on wire freestanding racks stationed next to fires or out-of-doors. But the rain and the dampness have made it impossible for anything to dry. It was becoming clear that either I was carrying an overly ripe hunk of Camembert somewhere in my backpack or it was time to wash and dry my clothes. We do wash our underwear every day—at least we women do. The men seem to remove their wet trousers and spend the rest of the evening walking around in their T-shirts and underpants. We women change into nightclothes and use the radiators to dry our panties and wet socks. After a while you can walk into any *gîte* and know who is already there by the panties drying on the radiator. I should mention these are not REI quick drying affairs or even my Victoria's Secret polka-dotted panties; no, these are lovely French silk panties with just the right amount of lace. French women believe that good lingerie is their right, as much a necessity of life as food and wine.

This is Saturday, June 1, and tomorrow I will set off from Castres. I have enjoyed regrouping and relaxing and the feeling of walking without the burden of my pack. After Castres, I will be on my own till I meet up with Ellen (Ellen, the cousin of a friend of mine, is an American living in Europe. We have never actually met but we have chatted on the Internet and it will be interesting to walk with such an experienced hiker.) in Auch on June 11.

Maybe I have been long-winded enough for one entry. . . .
Barbara

Goodbye Marie-Claude. . . .

LETTER SEVEN
Why My Way Is Not Martin Sheen's Way
Castres to Toulouse
June 7

More facts, figures, and why if you saw the film, *The Way*, you will understand that it is not what I am doing. Every year, 3,000 people walk the Arles Route. Every year, 25,000 (or 50,000 depending on who is counting) people walk the Le Puy-en-Velay route. And every year, 100,000 (or 250,000 depending on who is counting) people walk the route in Spain, the *Camino Francés*, the route Martin Sheen walked. Someone suggested I walk to eschew modernity—uh, err, not exactly. Eschewing modernity would be walking the Pacific Crest Trail or the Appalachian Trail, carrying all my freeze-dried meals, bathing in cold rivers, and sleeping alone in a tent. Let's be honest, I sleep and eat in *gîtes*, not in the crowded *refugios* depicted in Martin Sheen's *The Way*, but little hostels that hold six to 20 people, often only two to a room, a hot shower at the end of every day, a meal ranging from country French to downright gourmet, a bed and a blanket—sometimes even sheets and towels.

The last three *gîtes* were luxurious: an artists' house where every nook was a tableau of unique fabric art; a 1700's house built around a garden where four pilgrims were already sunning themselves when I arrived; and the most amazing, a castle and chapel that had been bought as a ruin 16 years ago and lovingly restored. It is run as a *donativo* (no set price you just slip money into a box to repay your hosts). What did we get in exchange for our *donativo*? A room for two with a private bath and Jacuzzi shower, fresh sheets and towels, a chance to wash our clothes and put them in a dryer (more joy than I can express), singing vespers at sunset in a little glass-walled chapel, a meal of homemade mushroom soup, roasted lamb and a fresh vegetable mélange, a green salad served with a platter of amazing local cheeses, and red wine. And the next day, a lovely breakfast. Nice huh? The castle sits atop a hill with views of the Pyrenees (the snow-covered Pyrenees where we are heading). The only thing you must do to stay here is walk the 30 km it takes to arrive, uphill—carrying everything on your back.

So if I am not eschewing modernity, why do I walk, why does anyone walk? The answers are as varied as the pilgrims. There are first and foremost the truly religious, Catholic or otherwise, who see their walk as a chance to honor and communicate with God. Last year, I walked briefly with a man from Vancouver, Canada. After we reached the town where I was stopping, he thanked me for the conversation and said he found it interesting as normally when he walked he only spoke with God. I assume I was a small comedown from his usual companionship.

Many people feel "called" to walk. I met Fernando from Asturias who was walking from Rome to Santiago as a thanks to God after he got a section of lung cut out from too much smoking (he showed us the scars at dinner). He is down to a pack a day, though I suspect God would feel a lot more gratified for his efforts if Fernando had stopped smoking altogether.

There are the once in a lifetime journeys from Rome or Poland or Amsterdam where pilgrims walk from their homes to Santiago and back! We met a singer from Venice who planned to walk from Venice to Santiago and back. His dream looked thwarted by swollen feet and a bad limp in Montpellier so I was surprised to come across Enrico in a small church during a storm. I may be surprised to meet up with him yet again.

There are the sportsmen. A couple of men from London were attempting the whole route in about half the time as anyone else—arriving at the *gîtes* at 7 PM and rising early to be off again. I wondered why they didn't just stay home and run around the track. They were grouchy and miserable and seeing nothing along the way but they were, as they were proud to say, very fast.

There are the *loups du Chemin* as I have discussed before who are questing after fresh meat.

There are the friends (or families) who solidify long relationships by walking together every year—a plan to complete the way to Santiago de Compostela in a ten-year period. It is an admirable bond and I am terribly jealous that such an opportunity does not exist for us in America. (I don't know the reason such trails with affordable shared sleeping accommodations do not exist. Is it because of our car culture, our litigious society, or our frontier heritage? Honestly I don't know.) There are friends I would love to invite for a yearly weeklong walk together. I met

six French women who had over the course of a dozen years walked for ten days each year. First they walked from Le Puy-en-Velay to Santiago, but when they arrived in Santiago they thought, "Why stop?" They began the Arles route last year. Their only rule is no husbands, children, or boyfriends. They have walked through marriages, deaths, divorces, illnesses and relocations. Every year they meet, just the six of them, and they walk again.

There are the addicts who, once they discover long-distance walking, cannot imagine a better way to spend their vacations. I may be in danger of becoming one of these. Actually, I have become one of them. I suppose it is the pace, the luxury of seeing a place slowly rather than speeding by in a car. It may seem strange that I take weeks and weeks to see what others visit in a few days but it feels like the right amount of time to me.

And there are the lone walkers, of which I am definitely one, or attempt to be one (but often find myself not all that alone). I began alone after Marie-Claude but acquired an interesting younger woman from Washington (the only other American on the *Chemin,* I think) or at least acquired her until Sunday when she will take a side trip to Carcassonne and I will go on to Auch to meet Ellen. Susan is about 40, with long red hair and an easy disposition. She recently found God and has decided to go to divinity school after her walk. Like many first time walkers, she has terribly over-packed but the weight of her pack equalizes her walking speed to mine.

I should mention that walking with Susan is a bit like walking alone since her ears have been permanently embedded with ear buds from her iPhone and she listens to music or Podcasts continuously except when she can find Wi-Fi to text with her boyfriend. For me this is fascinating, but also a missed opportunity. If France has nothing else it has birds and so many bird songs. After the rain lets up the birds tentatively begin their crescendos almost timidly at first, a solo here, another one there, then a duet, maybe a quintet follows until a full andante chorus is underway with the cuckoos coming in for percussion. Being from California, many of these bird songs I have only heard on my Audubon clock and the cuckoo of cheap Bavarian clocks made in China. One day, the cacophony of sound convinced me I was inside a clock gone mad with all the hours singing at once.

Second to the sound of the birds, is the lilting beauty of the butterflies. Even their names are beautiful—butterfly, *mariposa*, *farfalle*, *papillion*. But then of course we come to the German word, *schmetterlinge*—such a wonderful word sounding to my ear like a Brunnhilde helmet-wearing little creature darting about the forest screeching arias.

And third, especially this year, the beauty of the thousands and thousands of wild pink roses, lavender and blue irises, deep red corn poppies, purple orchids, white daisies, yellow brooms, and on and on. Purples, pinks, yellows, whites—fields and fields of brilliant color. The gift of too much rain is a gift we can be grateful for on sunny days and resent miserably on the days of wind and rain or when threading our way along paths so saturated with water that every step is like walking on dirty thick sponges.

Still, why walk alone and without the benefit of a distraction like ear buds or a chatty friend or well something, anything? Perhaps to test one's own companionship. If I cannot stand to be alone with myself, why should anyone else want to be with me? Perhaps to leave behind some of those metaphysical stones. I counted up (age has its downfalls) the would-of's, should-of's, could-of's of life—the friends, parents, spouse, and mentors who slipped from this life, fell off the trail so to speak. It is the weight of living on, not a bad thing to leave behind the accumulated sorrows and keep the joys.

And of course, walking alone is a chance to listen, really listen to the moment the world comes alive after the rains. To hear the wind in all its different tempos, tinkling leaves on the plane trees or howling out its vengeance against the world. To see the wind rippling through fields in light and dark shadows moving like a musical composition. To hear the silence of one's own breath and footsteps. Walking alone with only your thoughts for companionship (unless of course you have a Wi-Fi connection going with God which I do not, apparently, not even a single bar) is a unique joy, if you want it to be. Forgive my philosophical turn. I have been, indeed, walking alone.

And a little aside, as with all things French (as far as I can tell two French people will always provide at least three diverse opinions), I wanted to say Napoleon's plane trees only to read that there is controversy about whether Napoleon planted the tree-lined boulevards to shade his troops or Henry IV ordered trees planted to create straight boulevards. The trees are apparently under attack by drivers who object to deaths caused when they drive off the road and hit a tree, and cyclists who apparently drive off the bike paths and hit the trees from the other side but both cyclists and drivers agree the trees cause the deaths not the driving off of the roads.

Truth in advertising—I admit, at this moment, I am not walking alone. For that matter I am not even walking. I am sitting in a square in Toulouse where Susan and I decided to take a holiday from the *Chemin*. She, because it is her first time in Europe and she wants and needs time to absorb the big cities and me because the same right foot that got tendinitis last year is getting it again (not an old football injury but an old tango stiletto injury). I must rest my foot for a few days before I meet up with Ellen in Auch and head off to the Col du Somport in the Pyrenees. The Pyrenees and the pass over the Col du Somport should be the highlight of this adventure.

We are spending two days being tourists, or more accurately in my case, walking about until I find another place to sit. This has given me a lot of free time to contemplate the French since sitting in cafés is the ideal place to people-watch and form rash and unjust opinions. Some things amuse me, others not so much. First, these ultra-skinny, boy-hipped French women who spend their afternoons dawdling over gelato and *crème brûlée* have large-woman stores that start at size 38 (38 to 52). I am a size 4, which is a French size 38 and is the bottom size of the large-woman store—hmmppf! Second, in order for gay French men to distinguish themselves from the tight pants, ascot-wearing straight French men in their dress, they have to go very far out on the limb indeed! Third, how can Subway sandwich shops look so good here and yet retain that very unique, very American Subway odor—and be so popular. Fourth, I am not sure if the French are superb cooks or just have superb ingredients, but I spent the morning at the Toulouse covered market and I am not making guarantees but I think even I could produce a decent tasting meal if I shopped here. Fifth, *le Hamburger* when eaten with a knife and fork, well it just isn't a hamburger. At least the kids lining up outside the McDonald's franchise are getting that good old two-handed American grip. And if McDonald's moves the French bottom of the large-woman scale up from a size four to well maybe a size 8 or 10, I will personally wave the American flag.

This was sent Friday June 7 from Toulouse.

Viva le Hamburger,
Barbara

Letter Eight

Contradictions
Toulouse to Morlass
June 16

I am writing this in Auch. I do not know when I will finish or where I will be when I do. In Auch, I am impatiently waiting for my foot to return to normal size and for Ellen to arrive. In the *gîte* Sunday night, there was a couple, he French, she Canadian, a retired German man, and me (I guess I could be described as a retired American woman . . . hmmm). This *gîte* is only for sleeping with a small kitchen where pilgrims prepare their dinner and breakfast. The *gîte* is simple but with extraordinary views. We look directly onto the flamboyant gothic cathedral of Sainte-Marie with a Renaissance interior. I had never heard of flamboyant gothic either but trust me you know it when you see it—it is, well, flamboyant with arches and gables stretched and lengthened into a fanciful silhouette. It is a massive thing, 102 meters long and 35 meters wide, and especially beautiful in the moonlight.

Last night, as often happens, the Canadian/French couple bought enough food for everyone and we shared a lively dinner. During dinner, the priest led a tour of what I assume were parishioners to see how their money was being spent. They made small talk with us at dinner before moving on to see where we slept. I felt just a bit like a zoo animal on display but also grateful that these accommodations were provided.

The next morning, I repaid the favor of our dinner by waking early and walking the 30-minute round trip to the one open *boulangerie* so we could have warm bread with our morning coffee. I didn't like being left behind when they set off even though it was still raining and my foot still swollen. First contradiction—my anxiousness to begin walking again despite the size of my foot.

Second contradiction is Auch itself. An attractive city, on the river Gers—its banks lined with plane trees, a rich history from Nostradamus to the Musketeers, and many cafés (Gascony is known for its food), but I do not understand a culture with so many great perfumes, wines, and foods all depending on your sense of smell, but not noticing the *caca de chien*. Here in Auch, it is not just that no one cleans up after Fifi, even the café owners let people sit within two feet of an aroma that cannot be described as a perfume—no matter how much good Gascogne wine you consume.

Third contradiction is the American Jeans store. Unfashionable jeans-related clothing and high-calorie American fast food have droves of teenagers lined up to buy. Is it possible for us to make the French both fat and badly dressed? Kind of puts a smile on your face doesn't it?

Fourth contradiction was Monday night's misbehaving Parisian. Once again we shared a dinner (this time it was an opinionated Irishman, a chubby Parisian businessman, and a sweet-natured woman from Orleans, oh and me—the retired American woman) and once again I got up early to walk to the *boulangerie*. While I was out, the Parisian businessman took my bottle of milk meant for our *café avec lait chaud* and made one enormous *chocolat chaud* (hot chocolate). When I returned with the bread, I asked what happened to the milk? He said he thought it was for *nous* (us) so he drank all of it. What part of *nous* (us) became only *moi* (me)? Does it matter that one morning we drank our coffees black? No, of course not. The contradiction is my romantic belief that pilgrims always act for the common good. Sigh. . . .

Fifth contradiction is our pace. I flew thousands of miles to become an escargot—a snail moving at a snail's pace carrying my home on my back. All around us the world flies past while we slog through mud and rain, over hills and mountains, and every once in a while turning up in busy villages where we are reminded that the pace of the world is not ours. Cook us in garlic and butter and serve immediately.

This may be an excellent place to stop reading this letter if you find religious stuff boring or offensive or both.

Sixth contradiction is my ongoing attachment to Catholicism—the religion of my childhood. Why does Catholicism even matter to me? I have bigger fish to fry philosophically such as the existence of an external spiritual force, one that seems to be chatting up quite a few other folks on this *Chemin*. The Irishman in our *gîte* (yes, same night as the rude Parisian) declared only

devout Catholics, such as himself, had a right to walk the *Chemin*. God love the Irish, or in this case, God love him.

Still I must admit, I did try bargaining with God over this existence question. I suggested that if He did exist, maybe He could prove it by stopping the rain? That's when it started to hail. Cute.

Seventh contradiction is Catholicism and women. Here's the thing, the Marian culture is alive and well in France with many churches dedicated to the Virgin Mary (like *Notre-Dame* in Auch and Toulouse and of course, Paris). I grew up in the Marian culture, that is, we prayed almost exclusively to Mary to intercede for us with God . . . a sort of ask-mom-to-ask-dad thing. So, I feel comfortable with these French churches.

But then there are these little, ah, hiccups in Catholicism, like the new pope—yeah the good guy pope from Argentina—scolding the US Catholic nuns for spending too much time with the poor and the sick, and not enough time protesting abortion and gay marriage. I really like these nuns. I have always liked nuns—growing up in the 50's, nuns were the only women I knew who actually had independent thoughts. And apparently they still do. (I know this is not the image many of you have of nuns but trust me they can be a very feisty bunch. I was not the only little girl from that era who wanted to either be a nun or a ballet dancer.) Ok, I have vastly abbreviated the argument but I do not think I am misinforming. Whenever these nuns want to start their own church (and I get over my little theist blip) I'm joining.

All this Catholic stuff is on my mind because of visiting so many churches in Toulouse and Auch. In Toulouse, the *Basilique Notre-Dame de la Daurade* is one of many churches with a venerated *Vierge Noire* (Black Madonna). In fact, France has over 200 of Europe's 500 Black Madonnas. As far as I can tell, the explanation of a Black Madonna has more to do with the person explaining than anything else.

- A Catholic who prefers simplicity: The Black Madonna is a product of aged wood or smoke from candles.

- Traditional Catholic: Black Madonnas were painted black under the influence of St. Bernard of Clairvaux (1090 – 1153), who associated the phrase, "I am dark, but comely" (Song of Solomon 1:5) with the Virgin Mary.

- New Age: A guru chooses judicially from the traditions of the Knights Templar and the Cathars to create a satisfying woman-empowering story. Incomplete, but empowering.

- Historically Minded: There is a connection between churches containing Black Madonnas and churches built on top of primitive sites. The *Vierge Noire* has a strong resemblance to goddesses such as Isis suckling Horus. No explanation of what Isis is doing in the center of a Catholic altar.

Hundreds of non-fiction and fiction books are devoted to the origins and mysteries of the Black Madonna. Whether one believes the Black Madonnas originate with Isis and her immaculately conceived child Horus, were created in medieval times or are merely darkened due to candle smoke, their existence throughout France (one fourth of all of Europe's) is an intriguing mystery.

By the by, most of the Black Madonnas are replicas. During the violent French Revolution, the *Vierges Noires* were destroyed with cries of "death to the Egyptian goddess" (well at least you know where the French reformers stood on the question).

Bottom line: your guess is as good mine. The various histories of the *Vierge Noire* are documented, argued over, and as far as I can tell, unresolved.

But there she is right in the middle of the altar, replacing the dying Christ on the cross. The first time I saw a Black Madonna was in the cathedral in Le Puy-en-Velay—the start of last year's route. She was this little black doll, with a baby's face (Jesus/Horus) coming out of the middle of her robe—a robe. When I say little, I mean no more than two feet and looking, well, very much like she was borrowed from antiquity, which she very likely was.

Now, juxtaposition the veneration of the *Vierge Noire* and the Marian church with Auch's Renaissance windows and bas-reliefs of Adam and Eve. The face of the serpent and the face of Eve are the same face. Those Renaissance Catholics (you can find this in other Renaissance art such as the Adam and Eve paintings of Bugiardini or Massacio) placed the blame for all the world's problems squarely on the female. Eve wasn't merely tricked by the snake, Eve *was* the snake.

Catholicism and women—let's just say contradictions seven through seventy-nine. But then Catholicism is not my biggest question. Philosophically, I have to come to terms with the whole theist thing. Can I ever believe in God? I definitely have bigger fish to fry.

It is about one week until we reach the Col du Somport and it is not looking good. Two people died due to slippery conditions and the rain does not seem to want to abate. If I believed in God I suppose I could pray.

Finally sent Sunday June 16 from Morlass.

Best wishes to all. Let me know how you are doing. I've visited many interesting towns including Marciac—famous for its jazz festival. . . .

More about that in the next letter. . . .
Barbara

Adam and Eve (1425)
Masolino da Panicale
Image Courtesy of *Wikimedia Commons*

LETTER NINE
When Everything Floods
Morlass to Pau
June 21

I am beginning this on Sunday June 16 in Morlass. Ellen arrived in Auch and we began our journey together. She is a year or two older than me with short grey hair and a very opinionated disposition. We have stayed in some lovely towns and some not so lovely towns but with lovely people. From Auch we walked to Montesquieu, a town so near death that it is no longer even on life support. Everything but our small hotel and the church was closed—not temporarily closed but *fermé définitivement*.

At least the church was open. This trip has been different from last year as this year most churches have been locked which deprives me of one of my favorite past times—singing in what acoustically constitutes a very large shower stall. Last year there were three of us who always sang in the churches—a German woman, a French man, and me. When we happened to arrive at the same time we taught each other our songs so we could sing together.

In a church, I feel obliged to sing something religious which limits my repertoire to "Ave Maria," "Just a Closer Walk with Thee," "Amazing Grace," Girl Scout before-dinner graces, and the odd Christmas Carol. I have considered singing, "Come a Little Bit Closer You're My Kind of Man" to God but well . . . maybe He isn't.

Anyway, today was a 36 km day and very muddy. There were 8 km continuously of the kind of mud that sucks your boots off, clings to your shoes with a kilo of weight, and takes total concentration to stay balanced. Still, a slow motion fall into the muck is unavoidable. Everything in the mud is half speed. It is the oddest feeling to fall this slowly. You have so much time to think, "I am falling, I am falling, I am falling" yet, you can do nothing to stop the inevitable. After such a treacherous first day, Ellen was in an angry mood so going off to belt out a few tunes felt wonderful.

To add to our misery, the hotel could not have been more horrible. Well, it could have been the Bates Motel I suppose. Our room consisted of two beds (cots really), a sink and shower not behind a door, but against the wall facing the beds, (even the Bates Motel had a private shower but that didn't turn out so well did it?), and a bidet smack in the middle of the wall (toilet down the hall). Yeah, I know, a bidet in the middle of the room. My hiking partner's mood did not improve.

On the trail we had met Christian from Paris and there he was again, at our horrible hotel. We had all reserved *demi-pension* and of course we couldn't imagine what the food would be.

Christian and I did what any normal human being would do in such a circumstance—we went to the bar and ordered beers. Ellen eventually joined us and the three of us sat in a row facing the street doing our best imitation of three old Italians whiling away their afternoon on the sidewalk in front of the bar.

Then dinner began. It turned out we were at one of those restaurants I often read about where people come from afar for the food. Vegetable soup (At one time there apparently had been a veal leg involved. Vegetarians be warned, France is not an easy country for you.), quiche (vegetarians be warned again, there is a pig involved), a fricassee (don't even go there vegetarians), local sheep milk cheeses, and my new favorite dessert—a sort of prune/Armagnac gelato with extra Armagnac over the top. There was still a bidet in the middle of the room but well, after the wine and Armagnac it began to look sort of artsy.

A little aside about Italy and France and open bars. In Italy, if there are five houses in close proximity there will be a bar and the bar will be open and a row of old men will be sitting in front facing the street (old men in Italy come in sets of three or four and I suspect if the town does not have the requisite number they are imported from a neighboring village). There is always an open bar for coffee, wine, and some *prosciutto* and *pecorino*. The bar and the church are the centers of the community. Italian homes are comfortable but not necessarily grand and many large homes actually accommodate mama, sister and her husband and children, and maybe even an unmarried daughter. In France, homes are larger and apparently more self-contained and people feel less of a need for the communal life. Moreover, many of these villages have become no more than Parisian retreats with fewer and fewer full-time residents. The consequence for us pilgrims is to arrive at French villages midday with nothing, absolutely nothing, open. No people are on the streets. Even the dogs and cats hide behind closed doors. The shops and the *mairie* (city offices) are all closed between noon and 3 or 3:30, the bars are nonexistent or closed, and everyone is home having lunch *en famille*.

As long as I am on this tangent, Ellen gets grouchy if she cannot eat regularly. Part of our pilgrim planning now is to know when we can next buy food. Shops, including food shops, are closed from noon till 3:30, all day Sunday, and Monday mornings. *Patisseries* and *boulangeries* are closed on Sundays and Mondays except for one open in the morning to provide that day's bread. Towns without their own *boulangerie* and without a store functioning as a *dépôt de pain* (literally, a bread depot) have an early morning truck that arrives, honks, and everyone comes out in their nightdress to buy bread. I have seen truck drivers pass a baguette or two through open kitchen windows and front doors left slightly ajar. I imagine if one day one of the older folks is not seen buying bread someone goes to check on them.

I have more than once arrived in a town on a Sunday to a *gîte* with only a *coin cuisine* and made a dinner of dried figs and almonds. For Ellen this is a serious problem. She has a favorite phrase she often uses, "This is making me unhappy" and one thing that makes her unhappy is not being able to regularly eat. So now there is careful strategizing and mapping out of food sources. For example, on Saturday we're to sleep in a town without any stores, restaurants or bars and the *gîte* has no food so my walking mate must buy and carry enough food on Friday to last her until dinner Sunday night. Since I want to avoid listening to her complaints, I find I am now participating in worrying about whether or not she has enough food.

Well, back to the journey. The next day we walked to the very large and beautiful plaza of Marciac (reminiscent of Sonoma but much bigger) famous for its three-week summer jazz festival and yes, I am tempted to come back in July. Anyone want to rent a place with me for next year? We stayed in a *gîte* run by an Algerian couple. The wife's first reaction to learning I was American was; "Oh, you hate me because I am Muslim. All Americans hate Muslims." Sigh.

After dinner and after Ellen went to bed, the proprietress and I had the kind of talk you can only have when you lack language skills. There is a phenomenon that makes small talk impossible when you have no small-talk words. You get right down to speaking about what is on your mind. We talked about Shiites and Sunnis, the United States post-9/11, Middle Eastern women (an impressive force to be reckoned with), and about the difference between Muslims in France and Muslims in Algeria. Like all immigrants, the French Muslims often preserve a past that no longer exists in the country they left.

The next day Ellen and I passed through Maubourguet. We stopped for a walk around the village before heading off to our country *gîte* in Vidouze. The *gîte* accommodates eight, but no other pilgrims arrived so we had the entire house, garden, and swimming pool to ourselves. The plum tree in front of our door was at least five meters across and held a New York City of birds (well maybe only an Omaha, but certainly a lot of birds). There was a cacophony of bird songs till dark when the frogs took over the symphony.

Next, we walked to Anoye and another *gîte* with a beautiful garden. In this part of France rose bushes grow out of any crack in the sidewalk and bloom from every stem. There are literally more blooms than leaves. I have never seen anything comparable. I admit more than a tinge of jealousy as I nurse and carefully tend my Northern California rose bushes—watering, fertilizing, controlling diseases—in hopes of getting a few blooms in our relatively dry climate. I feel like Alice in Wonderland with so many blossoms and bushes that tower over me but with no wicked queen telling me to paint them red. Of course we can thank the rain.

So about the rain, the abundant rain. There is now a storm, a week-long storm, a very very big storm. I suggested we wait it out in Pau as the trails are impassable. Pau is a surprisingly beautiful and comfortable city with a greater percentage of gardens than any other city in Europe, views of the Pyrenees, a castle where King Henry IV was born, medieval architecture, churches of course, and the Gave de Pau River. The rain has caused us to be behind our original schedule but it has also placed us here just in time for the countrywide Solstice Music Festival (June 21) where every plaza and street corner becomes a feast of music.

But what you may have seen on the news is that since we arrived, the Gave de Pau flooded here and in Lourdes. I had never seen a rushing river overflowing its banks before; if the word were not so overused I would say it was awesome—terrible and awesome. Although I was taking all this rain as a personal message from God, I figure when He floods His own mother's grotto, he's got bigger fish to fry than me. I seriously considered stopping my journey but decided instead to go on, onward to the Pyrenees on Saturday. Oh, the music festival will also go on though most likely under umbrellas.

What I learned this week is that sometimes everything floods—the rivers, the houses, the emotions of the trail. Sometimes it is all just too much. Ellen is a kind of exhausting flood. She is about my age but has much more money, vast experiences long-distance walking and disappointed. Her displeasure exhausts me. I feel like a long-eared puppy bounding through flowers chasing butterflies while a bored human waits for me to finish my romp. My essential joy annoys her. Others' happiness when you are not happy is like Chinese water torture.

She announces she is quitting every day, quitting for good and heading back home (and every day I listen in silence hoping she will indeed return to her home in Austria),

France was hit by storms more akin to the tropics in the summer of 2013 that put much of the country on alert. The southwest of the country, especially the Pyrénées region, was particularly badly hit, with the famous Catholic shrine of Lourdes almost submerged under the flood waters. Paris was also hit by fierce electric storms. (*The Local*)

but now she has decided to go on. I do not believe she is an essentially unhappy woman but I do not know her outside of this experience. She is here at my invitation so I would not feel right asking her to walk alone. I remember Marie-Claude's patience with me and I try to undo Ellen's rudeness with kindness, but when are we acting kindly, because we are kind, or when we are just cowards?

Her constant comparisons and complaints have caused me to ponder: "is this how we age?" Is everything not what it was before? Is this hike not as good as another, this sunset not as beautiful, this friend or lover not what they were before? Since we are not who we were, not as good as we were before, is nothing as good as before? Do we somehow lose the joy of the moment as we assess and compare and feel disappointment in everything we see? Nothing is as it was because "was" is gone and never to return.

There are people who are never quite here. They are some place better. They are comparing this to that and that to everything that went before. For me, this moment is new and exciting but then my pleasures are simple. Are my pleasures simple because I do not have Ellen's money and cannot demand greater luxury and greater service? That is the question of the chicken or the egg I suppose.

I don't know the answer, but here is my version of raindrops on roses and whiskers on kittens. It is less poetic but remember Maria was singing on mountaintops in a blue dress with a white apron and I am wearing hiking boots and covered with mud:

- Pristine views of the snow-covered Pyrenees
- The two cherries Stefan left for us on the picnic table next to the trail, knowing we would probably stop there. A sweet goodbye.
- A dry trail without mud
- Quiet
- Butterflies leading the way
- Bird and frog serenades
- A breeze on sweaty arms on a warm day
- A warm fire on a cold rainy day
- A hot shower after a long walk
- Clean clothes
- Socks that don't smell
- Brilliant colors streaming from stained glass church windows
- A field of blue and yellow Johnny Jump-Ups
- A single perfect rose bud
- Singing
- Armagnac on gelato or maybe just Armagnac or maybe just alcohol

I am finishing this on Friday, June 21, in Pau where everything and nothing happened. I am not sure when there will next be Wi-Fi. Saturday, I begin walking toward the Col du Somport. I should be there by mid-week. I have accepted that the Col du Somport may be impassable. I will walk if it is only muddy and difficult but not if it is dangerous. I will be disappointed if I must take the bus but I will find new things to add to my happiness list and I will continue to look for that bigger fish I want to fry.

Missing all of you very much,
Barbara

LETTER TEN

Getting Lost to Get Found
Pau To Canfranc to Urdos
June 28

I did it! I walked the Col du Somport on the *Chemin*. I walked from Urdos over the pass and on to Canfranc in Spain. Then I got on a bus and came back to Urdos in France.

"You did what? Barbara, haven't you been making this big deal, ahem, out of getting over the pass all this time and then you turn right around and go back to France? Are you nuts?"

First let me say I have not changed my itinerary; I am still going to Puente la Reina in Spain, but the Pyrenees, ah the Pyrenees. I needed more. The Pyrenees and I were not quite done with each other. They are in a word, well, in a word, hmmm, I was going to use the word beautiful but merely beautiful looks so puny compared to what I am looking at right now so I looked for a synonym and found splendiferous! Not normally in my vocabulary but neither are the Pyrenees. The Pyrenees are splendiferous!

I have tried to photograph them but the pictures do not capture being encapsulated by the mountains nor the sounds and movement. If I were a poet or musician maybe I could create the music that captures them. But I am not, so I will do my best with simple words. Like splendiferous!

Before the Col du Somport, we walked for several days in a long valley in the Pyrenees, sometimes on the trail and sometimes forced onto roads due to rivers that could not be forded or trails covered in landslides. Whether on roads or trails, we had the pleasure of the Pyrenees.

So let me explain—first the mountains themselves. On the French side they jut straight out of the earth with sheer faces and jagged edges against the sky. Unlike other mountain ranges that are uniform and almost blend one

into the other (especially for a one-eyed girl like me who often cannot distinguish one mountain from another and sees only a single skyline), each mountain of the Pyrenees has an individual look and color. One is grey and snow-capped without any vegetation and with clouds creating horizontal patterns across its drab face. The mountain to its right is lush green, undulating with yellow flowers. The one to the left is forested except for an enormous oval of deep red rock (Garumnian). The mountains are limestone, shale, siltstone, argillite, Garumnian. The mountains are red, grey, blue, brown, green. The mountains are forested, barren, snow-covered, flowering. Each mountain seems jealous of the other's beauty and feels a need to outshine.

The snow is melting and waterfalls begin above the clouds, pull away from the vertical facings, and end far below in the turbulent rivers. Every crevice is bleeding water as if a heart within the mountain was pumping—water shoots out like a cut artery. The sound of the rivers is a constant background rumble and when standing next to any river, one must shout to be heard. It is a sustained roar announcing itself, threatening its banks, demanding respect. The rivers are a churning frothing white. When I think of rapids, I imagine a river with calm waters interrupted by white water. Every meter of these rivers is a stage four or five rapid. There are no calm waters.

The mountains, the waterfalls, the rivers are majestic in their enormity and energy. In contrast the rainfall has encouraged a soft sweetness all around. Hillsides and meadows are carpeted with deep red and purple orchids; gentians show off in rows of blue, yellow and white, endless fields of yellow marguerites, a meadow of nothing but purple irises, and trails lined with broom, century plants, bears ear, butterwort, wild roses, rhododendrons and on and on and on. Streams appear out of nowhere between yellow and purple flowers. Deep greens, yellow greens, and lime greens push down the hills in random patterns. It is breathtaking.

Of course the butterflies cannot resist such color and beauty and they are everywhere, closing their brilliant wings to become nothing more than green and brown leaves. They are yellow and orange trimmed in deep brown, pale blue like a winter sky, and white with black designs, zebra patterned, spotted, striped. I have no idea why artists think angels have plain white wings. Surely if there are angels they must have the Technicolor wings of a butterfly.

Nature's beautiful murderers are out in force. Cuckoos lay their giant eggs in songbird nests where the Rosemary's Baby of a stranger's child eventually murders the natural children. Ivy wraps itself artistically around tree trunks creating a fashionable overcoat as it slowly destroys. Moss lays waste to its overly generous host. Nature's Pac-man (now that's an old computer game reference) of bigger eating smaller leaves traces of death along the trail.

We have come upon rutting wild boars, marmots, lizards, and all sorts of eagles and birds of prey. I joked that the bearded vulture circling us was waiting for its chance until I learned last month one of the hikers fell to her death in the torrential rainfall and was indeed consumed—all that was left was scraps of clothes and her shoes. It is not a joke I will make again.

There are the domestic animals being pastured on hillsides (transhumance). You hear their multi-toned bells reverberating down the mountains long before you see them. Herds of goats follow hikers like a class of eager first graders until the dogs decide it is time to corral them back. Sheep look smug, like they know something we do not (and perhaps they do). Sheep also participate in something best described as formation marching. I know about this. I played in my high school band. The sheep are better, but I have no idea why they walk in these long single file lines creating figure eights on the hillsides. And the *blonde d'Aquitaine*, a white cow that is, as far as I can tell, not a cow at all but a mountain with eyes and horns. When these little hillsides decide to move you do not want to be in their way. They are as much a part of the enormity of the Pyrenees as the snow-covered mountains and precariously perched outcroppings that threaten to turn hikers into a vulture picnic.

Of course it is spring, so there are baby goats and sheep that are still trying to stand, just-born horses, and donkey kindergartens. We came across a three-day old Shetland pony that looked exactly like one of those tiny stuffed animals one wins at the fair by throwing rings over bottles.

So you see, I had to come back. I had to spend more time in this startling contrast between sweet serenity and energetic force. Between the silence filled only with rippling aspen leaves and bird songs and the thunderous tympani rumble of the rivers and falls. This is nature giving you everything it has got, putting on its spring show spectacular. And all those weeks of rain have created this, so it is not just a great pleasure, it is an earned pleasure.

I will leave on Saturday for Spain. Ellen has returned home and I am again on my own—this time I will be in a country where I have never hiked and probably speak even less Spanish than my meager French. I can expect only the unexpected and that has been one of the lessons of the *Chemin*.

A person plans and plans, and still things are not quite as expected. Then one does not plan, in fact one gets lost as I did last year when I found Suzanne and Peter (or rather Suzanne found me). Last year, I accidentally took a variant and Suzanne found me at least ten kilometers away from the proper trail. She and Peter took me in for the night and drove me back to where I should have been in the morning—but only after a most interesting conversation about God, art, and the political role of the US in Europe. This year I spent four hours and 16 km walking in circles not realizing that I was giving Marie-Claude time to catch up to me so we could walk together. Being lost gives us a chance to find something for which we did not know we were looking.

Suzanne and Peter

Sometimes we meet ourselves when we are lost. We learn who we really are, not who we thought, but rather who, when tired and possibly afraid, we can be. We find strength we did not know we had. We find solutions to problems. It sounds like smarmy new age nonsense but there is a discovery when one is pushed to their limits, when one is alone, when nothing is familiar.

I always joked that I handle the world by complaining. Then I got a real complainer as a hiking mate. I realized I am actually a fixer. When faced with disaster, I fix it or adjust. When the road straight ahead is impassable, I find the alternate. When the *gîte* is not as expected, I enjoy what it is. That song, "Love the One You're With", may also apply to life, "love the life you've got".

One night I just started laughing as Ellen recited her litany of complaints. It was her complaint about the pillow being too big and making her unhappy that made me laugh and see the absurdity of this phrase. I couldn't explain my laughter to her but the expression, "this is making me unhappy" suddenly struck me as utterly ridiculous. When does one give power to a pillow or a mattress or the configuration of the toilet or even the rain to make us unhappy? Of course, I came very close to giving my unhappy hiking partner the power to make me unhappy. I came very close to becoming lost in Ellen's unhappiness.

Although Ellen is an ardent long-distance walker, she does not like *gîtes* or the pilgrim lifestyle. Of course there is no need to be a pilgrim and walk a *Chemin* if walking appeals to you. All of Europe is creating more and more long distance trails. Every country has a version of them, even Turkey.

Most long distance walkers are just walkers but *Chemin de St-Jacques* hikers refer to themselves as Pilgrims. Yes, I know, it is rather precious. It is part of the tradition of the *Chemin*. People wish us *"Bon Chemin"*, *"Bonne Route"*, but mostly *"Bon Courage"*. We thank them for their good wishes. We ask strangers for help and we admit we are lost. Accepting their help is for some of us even more difficult than the asking.

A few days ago I became lost and knee deep in mud on a hillside. As I came down the hill, I saw another hiker in the distance. I chased him down and asked him to guide me to my destination. That was Martin from Austria who has turned up again and again since that first day, including appearing out of nowhere and handing me a piece of Spanish almond candy as I reached the top of the Col du Somport. Maybe he does not even exist and if I looked more carefully I would find luminously colored butterfly wings tucked under his backpack.

This was sent Friday June 28, from Urdos. Tomorrow I leave (again) for Spain.

I hope all of you are well and having a splendiferous day,
Barbara

LETTER ELEVEN

Everything Is Different In Spain
Urdos to Canfranc to Jaca
July 1

What a difference a mountain makes! To begin, the mountain itself is different. The Pyrenees slope downward on the Spanish side and lose that pronounced vertical facing of the French side. Put more simply, the Alpine ski resorts are on the Spanish side and the Nordic ski resorts are on the French side. The Spanish slopes are gray and red with less and less vegetation until finally there is only scrub brush and shortened trees. Spain has had the same unusual rainfall so there is grass in the fields and periodic bursts of red corn poppies, but there is an austere economy of vegetation. The rivers are running full and fast and segments of the trail have become shallow rivers, but no mud. I know this sounds ridiculous but the ground is so hard there is maybe a half-inch of surface mud but no sink-your-boot-into deep mud. The trail is consistently rock and gravel—not the easiest terrain for a girl with a bad foot.

Everything is different. It is hot and dry; the kind of dry that when a car drives by, the dust stays in the air for a good ten minutes as though it had nothing better to do than float. (Well really dust has nothing better to do because when it's not dust, it is really just dirt isn't it?) It is hot enough to finally wear a T-shirt and break out that giant tube of 50-strength sun block I have been carting around for seven weeks. Those of you who know about my battles with basal cell skin cancer know sun is not my friend. It is amazing to me that by simply walking over a mountain the air should change so drastically.

Everything is different. Of course the people have changed. Uh, duh Barbara, you're in a different country—language, look, attitude. Gone is our *"Bon Courage"* and replaced, well, replaced with very little. I understand that on the *Camino de Santiago* the pilgrims tire of wishing each other *"Buen Camino"* but this is still a quiet road until Puente La Reina where the Arles *Chemin* joins the *Camino de Santiago*; I do pass other hikers and let's face it Spanish men will flirt with a rock so a *"Buenos Días"* is often responded to with a smile and a compliment from the men. And I am not complaining. When you are 63, wearing a front and back pack, sweaty hiking clothes, a cap pulled low across your forehead, and someone is willing to pay you a compliment, well that is just fine with me. I can even believe it for a minute or two. Why not? It is much more difficult to get a smile from the women. They return a look reminiscent of the derisive downcast face of a flamenco dancer.

Everything is different. Even the bells. I have been remiss in not mentioning the bells. Bells have been a consistent music of this trip. The *gîtes* are often located next to or even within monasteries and churches. The church bells ring every hour (really, every single hour, 12 rings at midnight, 1 ring at 1 AM, and so forth, this light sleeper can attest) often just announcing the hour, usually twice in succession in case you didn't get the count the first time. The bells call the people together for mass with an urgent insistent ringing. I have heard bells solemnly proclaiming a death. The slow ringing of a single bell, the death knell, reverberates through your skin. You hear the death. You feel the death.

Now in Spain, even the bells are different. Here multiple bells play more tuneful songs from their belfries. Little melodies at every hour. I read that the life of a peasant in long ago times (or perhaps not so long ago) was lived within the radius of 15 miles from the village, ruled by the church bells, which must have been a source of great comfort and fear. Fifteen miles—your entire world, and church bells were your Wi-Fi, Google and television rolled into one.

But these are not the only bells of this journey. The pastured animals all have their own set of bells. The lead cow, sheep, or goat has the larger more important bell and probably a neck ache—the reward for being a natural-born leader. Where herds are pastured together, every animal gets a smaller less impressive bell than the lead bell but a sound unique to that herd. The pastured animals with their myriad of different tones and rhythms create their own musical counterpoint.

I have not yet heard Spanish herd bells. Perhaps without the lushness of vegetation multiple herds are not pastured together.

Everything is different. One thing not to worry about in Spain is food and drink. As far as I can tell, the many bars and restaurants are always open. Unlike the French, there are no assigned times to eat. The restaurants near my *refugio* in Jaca open at noon and serve continually until midnight. People are sitting there at 1 PM and still sitting there at 5 PM (often the same people). The stores are open even on Sunday. The only problem I have had with food is finding portions that fit my appetite—the portions here are enormous! Even the chocolate bars look as though the jolly green giant went off his diet of vegetables and decided to indulge in sweets.

Everything is different, even the vegetation . . . yeah, about that scrub brush I mentioned earlier. I have not previously brought the subject up, the delicate subject of nature's call. Now I don't know if most of you realize it but we Americans live in a port-a-potty world. If you go for a hike there will be a port-a-potty if not an entire restroom at the start of the trail. If you stop at a rest stop there is a port-a-potty. There is, as far as I can remember, never a picnic table, never a drinking fountain, never a festival without the requisite port-a-potty.

Well we're not in Kansas anymore, Dorothy. Here you can find picnic tables, viewing sites, forest rest houses where you can spend the night, trail markers for dozens of varying length walks, but never will you find a port-a-potty or any other type of restroom facility. It's every man or woman for themselves. This was not a problem on the French *Chemin* as the trees were large and the brush thick. You needn't step far off the trail to find total privacy.

Spain looks to be whole other kettle of fish (there must be a better metaphor but it's escaping me right now). The trees are spindly and the brush scarce. Even though I am thinner, I am not yet thin enough to hide behind these skinny trees (but I may have dropped one size under the French large-woman stores).

And okay, this whole thing about losing weight on the trail (She writes this while munching a very tasty piece of cheesecake after lunch.), my unhappy walking mate was obsessed with whether we were losing weight. Really, spas are a much more attractive way to lose weight than walking in mud. At a spa they carefully put mud on your face, you don't have to drag it around all day on your clothing and shoes. Still, American women always ask, "Did you lose weight?" My answer is: I do not know. If you walk this much every day muscles do tighten. Last year, at the end of my walk, I went to Bordeaux for a few days. I couldn't help but notice all the French women were wearing what appeared to be spray-on orange (skin tight) pants. I thought to myself, "I just walked 500 miles. I could wear skin tight orange pants". So I tried some on. Zipped right up. Fit like a glove. Then I went to the three-way mirror in the center of the store and looked behind and the young store clerk saw exactly what I was seeing and said in her cutest little French

accent, "*vous* could always wear ze tunic". Yes even after 500 miles I do not have French little-boy hips, I have Italian big-girl hips. And one thing I immediately liked about Spain is apparently the only ones here with little-boy hips, are indeed, little boys.

American men ask, "How far did you walk" and "How many miles per day?" I can answer the men's question—sort of. Arles to Puente la Reina on the GR 653 is 859 or 900 km depending on which guide book or web site you use. Even that isn't accurate, as sometimes I walked on the road, which would make it shorter. Sometimes I walked backwards (My remarkable inverted sense of direction did not improve just because I was walking across France.). So somewhere in the vicinity of 550 miles, more or less, when I finally arrive. The number of miles per day also varied. A short day is 12 or so miles. A normal day is about 20 miles. An ambitious day is 25 to 30. There are of course pilgrims who walk my ambitious day every day. The question for me now is how far can I walk over these rocky trails with my gimpy foot?

How bad is the foot? Well, the beggars outside of churches have stopped asking me for money and are looking at me like potential competition. Really, what separates a pilgrim from any homeless person in the big cities? Well we have our scallop shells hanging from our packs. Normally my scallop shell is tucked into a pocket except when I am in a big city and I want to distinguish myself from derelict homeless people seeking shelter who have no choice, as I am a derelict homeless person seeking shelter *with* choice.

Why a scallop shell? There are dozens of explanations but the shells are as iconic of the Way as the golden arches of McDonald's or the swish of Nike. Here are two explanations I have heard.

1. After St Jacques' death, his disciples shipped his body to the Iberian Peninsula to be buried. Off the coast, a heavy storm hit and the body was lost at sea. After some time, the body washed ashore undamaged, covered in scallops.

2. After St, Jacques' death, his body was transported by a ship with no crew (yep that's right, no crew) to Spain. There was a wedding taking place as Jacques' ship approached. The groom's horse spooked, and horse and rider plunged into the sea. Through a miracle, the horse and rider emerged from the water alive and covered in shells.

It may be simply that the Galician Coast is covered in scallop shells. As far as I can tell the main advantage of having the shell is that people are nicer to you when they think you have a choice about being homeless.

Everything is different. I have not been the perfect guest in Spain. On my first day I had a bit of an argument with the authorities of the small town where I was staying. Let me back up and explain why I was staying in the small town.

There was a variant to the Spanish 65.3 that was slightly longer and supposed to be a quieter route to the next town about eight or so kilometers away. The variant was indeed well marked but it was a very hot and rocky trail. Just as I should have been arriving to the next town and when I had completely run out of water, I discovered that due to the rains, the footbridge I needed to cross had been damaged and was blocked to pedestrians. The river was running far too high and fast to ford. So, yes, eight km back to the little town where I decided to stay the night. On the way back, I met two other pilgrims who were set on fording the river (eventually they too came back). I went to the authorities and explained we needed a sign before someone does something foolish and is hurt or killed. The authorities asked why? I said because it was a long hot walk and once there you are tempted to be foolish, and if there were just a sign at the beginning of the variant, the temptation could be resisted. They looked at me quizzically. I had the feeling the Spaniards thought that it was a sort of natural selection if people were dumb enough to ford the river. I lost the argument but I did get up early the next morning and walk out to the trailhead to put up a sign.

Everything is different. One last difference worth mentioning: the inside of the churches. The Spanish have no problem portraying the gruesomeness of the Old and New Testaments, in full and almost lurid detail. No soft peddling Christianity with the Marian culture of France. Here you are reminded again and again that Christ suffered and died for your sins. Horribly. Painfully. Horrifically. He died because of you. And you owe him! Big time!

I have spent more time this year than last going to Mass, in large part because so many churches have been locked and the only way to see the inside was to go to mass. The last Mass I went to in France was in Sarrance, a small town in the Pyrenees. I went because I wanted to see . . . drum roll please . . . the Black Madonna on which the monastery had been founded. A shepherd and a fisherman found the stone head of this particular Black Madonna. She did look suspiciously prehistoric.

Everything is the same but everything is now different. In a Catholic Church when the candles and incense are burning, when nuns sing vespers or the priest a Gregorian chant, when colored lights stream across the altar from the stained glass windows, and organ music fills the vaulted ceiling with sound, I am not ashamed to admit that I can be spun around and feel a sense of peace and belonging. This is the very air I breathed as a child. But, and I do not say this lightly or happily, I do not belong. It is not my church.

The Catholic Church of my childhood taught me not just the beauty but also the immense power of art, architecture, and music. I learned from the nuns that women could think for themselves and they taught me that we have an intrinsic responsibility for others. I learned the importance of being still and of meditating. I was also a child and I believed in the priests and the rules, and that following the rules was important but I realize now that the one thing I did not believe in was a God or a god or god(s). I believed in the church but never quite in God. That is what I am still seeking. I am still asking, "Can I be a theist?" So Catholicism, thank you. I will always be happy to meditate in your churches but I still have bigger fish to fry, and you are not the fry pan for me.

This was written on Monday, the first of July in Jaca, Spain where I attended mass in the nearly 1000-year old cathedral of St. Peter the Apostle.

Et cum spiritu tuo,
Barbara

LETTER TWELVE

Of Vultures and Butterflies
Jaca to Obanos
July 7

Spain continues to appeal, disappoint, and amaze. Day after day, I experience the important differences. I had expected the French GR 653 to change to the Spanish 65.3. I expected the language to change. I expected the food to change. I even expected the local people to change but it would still be the same walk, the same pilgrims, the same goals. Everyone would be heading in the direction of Santiago. How different could that be? Where to begin!

As I already mentioned, the landscape is different. Here, there are great expanses of cultivated and wild lands as far as the eye can see. It makes sense that "vista" is a Spanish word. I think of Spain as horizontal and France as vertical (at least the parts I have been walking). The flat-topped hills remind me of the Arizona geology of my childhood, but with completely different flora: yellow broom, purple thistle, grasses ranging from golden reds, pale blue, and an almost black green. No cacti, but the scratches on my arms are a testament to the height and thickness of the thistles.

Overhead, we are entertained with circling Imperial eagles, vultures and hawks. After what I read happened to that English pilgrim, I look upon them with true deference and respect. I had never seen vultures circling in flocks before. I began this trip with pink flocks of flying flamingoes in the Camargue and am ending it with the white, red, black, brown Griffin and Egyptian vultures of Navarro.

Mostly though there is agriculture, fields of corn, wheat, melons, and squash. We walk on farm tracks between fields. It is a patchwork of yellows and greens broken only by small villages of red brick and even redder roof tiles or often only the ruins of a village. The church towers always retain that one last bit of height as they collapse in an edgy diagonal.

Sadly, we enter many towns through what one pilgrim described as the garbage shoot. Spain has improved greatly over what it was twenty years ago, but there is still a propensity to discard waste just over there, just over here, just out of sight. And maybe it doesn't matter as a portion of our walk could disappear depending on who wins the argument to expand a large reservoir. Many of the villages are simply ruins, being brought back to life with *refugios* (Spanish version of French *gîtes*) for pilgrims. These are slated to drown under the proposed reservoir. The uncertainty creates a half-hearted approach to construction.

From left to right: Escarlate, Amadeu,
Alberto, Barbara, Maite's father and Maite

When one is not looking up at the vultures one can look down at the butterflies. In Navarro, when the butterflies fold their wings they do not disappear into green or brown leaves but like a reversible jacket are showy on both sides. I assume this is because there are no leaves to disappear into, as plant life here is more spindly, prickly and reedy. I enjoy walking ahead and being the first to rouse the butterflies so that they may, as they did in France, lead my way down the path. So I can look up at the power of these carnivorous birds or down at the vulnerability of these fluttering wisps and I know I am standing just in-between.

There are also snakes, not many, or at least not many to an Arizonian. It is easy to think of Arizona in this part of the world. There is something so familiar yet like the landscape, somehow the same, but not. It has been a source of amusement to all of us that big burly Randy from London, with his great fear of serpents, practically tiptoes his way on the road to Santiago. I had to look this up but England apparently only has three types of snakes and three types of lizards and I suppose none of them hang out in London proper. He will surely end up with blisters on the balls of his feet if he can't settle down over this snake thing.

Randy from London, Karum from Atlanta, and Alberto from the Canary Islands were the first pilgrims I met in the Spanish *refugios*. These three friends, friendships met and made on the *Camino*, were the most unlikely threesome I could imagine. What they had in common was to be three young men on a journey. What they did not have in common was language, education, personality or religion, yet they were building a friendship out of shared experience.

There is much about Spanish *refugios* I could not imagine. The *refugios* are definitely an eye-opening experience (I could also say eye-popping but I won't go there.) In several *refugios*, the beds were chockablock next to each other. Everyone brings everything into the room so there is no effort to contain bedbugs, but more importantly, there is stuff everywhere and limbs everywhere, and breath everywhere. You may be familiar with the sorrows of someone's soles, long before you learn their name.

The number of toilets and showers has not so far been in relationship to the number of beds, so there is a certain amount of waiting, as patiently as possible, to use the facilities. Sharing a sink means learning how to smile and nod a greeting while brushing your teeth—the trick is to close your mouth over the brush and give a closed mouth smile so you don't foam like you have rabies. There are just a lot of people in a relatively small space and a bit of a test for this shy introvert—though meeting people feet first does eliminate some of the social challenges of conversation. A good opening line, "So, do your blisters hurt a lot?"

When there are twenty or fewer people in the *refugio*, it is still possible to cook a meal together and sit down at the outdoor table in a ruin of a village. One of the pilgrims, Amadeu from Valencia, prepared the most astonishing paella. How he did it with limited ingredients still baffles me. Amadeu and his wife Escarlata are flutists and I had the great pleasure of walking with them off and on for the next week (and eating more of Amadeu's excellent cooking). And no, for those of you asking, no, I did not participate in the cooking part of the experience. Someone has to wash dishes. Walking with Alberto and this group from Valencia has been a real pleasure despite our age differences. They are experienced *Camino* walkers who know and love the beauty of their country and their good humor is infectious.

Many *refugios* hold 60, 100, or 200 people. The numbers have increased geometrically as we approached the *Camino de Santiago*. It does feel like there must be the 250,000 pilgrims a year on the *Camino de Santiago* as I have recently been told. I do not know the correct number but suffice it to say it is a very different experience.

Those walking together on the Spanish *Camino de Santiago* often build groups of 20 or 30 friends who will bond and walk together. In short, this Spanish *Camino* is an incredible social experience. You cannot help but befriend, fall in love, and connect with people all marching in your same parade. Maybe it is the Catholic Burning Man with all the nudity but none of the overt sexuality—and of course it lasts for over a month. Alberto showed me a picture of at least 35 people entering Santiago together with the explanation, "They were all my friends". I believe they all were but it is a world apart from the two to six people who shared *gîtes* in France.

With this number of pilgrims, the trail sizes are worth mentioning. The Spanish trails have so far been almost all gravel, dirt, or tarmac roads—roads big enough for a car or your closest 35 friends. Unlike France, on this Spanish *Camino*, less than 10% of the *Camino* has been what one would call a trail. (Yes, I remember that France's narrow dirt trails turned into mud. Really, I haven't forgotten the mud.) I have spoken to several pilgrims and they tell me that most Spanish trails are like this even the *Camino del Norte*, which I was thinking of walking next year. I am not a fan of these surfaces but the size actually fits the extreme social aspect of the Spanish *Camino*.

Another difference is that I am meeting authentic trail addicts. Donald from Vancouver let us know within five minutes of our introduction that since May 1, he has walked 1,500 kilometers. Think about that. Granted I have been a bit lazy and only walked 900 kilometers since May 15, but wow, 1,500!

He never takes a day off, never deviates to visit churches, and sometimes walks 40 or 45 km a day. There is a feeling of one-upmanship amongst a certain group of pilgrim addicts. Certainly not the majority but these talkative types can dominate the table with their been-there done-that stories. It reminds one of how every microcosm of society has its die-hards. There are Civil War re-enactors, *Star Wars* fans, tango dancers, miniature train fanatics, improv performers, and on and on, who compress their world into something manageable where they can achieve top status.

Pilgrims can also be competitive about how little they spend. Not spending money has relatively little to do with whether the person can afford to spend money in "real" life. It is the game of not spending. It is the knowing where the cheapest *refugio* is and where to find the biggest cheapest pilgrim meal. Of course for some pilgrims this is a necessity but for many it is just another form of one-upmanship, or I guess in this case one-downmanship. And spending does matter. Pilgrims used to depend on the community for everything. Now many of these Spanish communities depend on what the pilgrims spend. We are an important industry in Spain's floundering economy.

Most pilgrims I have met in Spain are walking to Santiago this year, but more interesting to me is that almost everyone started in Spain or just on the border with Spain. Folks walking my route, the GR 653 (or Spanish 65.3), flew here from all over the world, took trains, and then a bus to the Col du Somport and did not even see the French Pyrenees or only from the window of a bus. I am not sure how it is they do not know that there are trails all over Europe connecting to the Spanish trails, which are in fact considered by everyone else in Europe, the start of the trail. I should mention I am suddenly in a world full of English speakers—from the States, Great Britain, Australia, etc.—another surprise. There are improv games where one person is not supposed to hear what the others are saying and so before the game begins they stand to the side tapping their ears and saying "lalalalaa" loudly so they cannot hear. People all around me seem to be repeating, "lalalalaa".

When they ask where I began my *Camino*, I tell them I started in Arles, France. They are bewildered that a trail starts outside of Spain. When they grasp that the trail really did begin in France, they dismiss this because France is too expensive and all French people are rude. If I tell them that the *gîtes* are affordable, they do not believe me. If I dare suggest French people are nice, even kind, they are even more incredulous. There is a mantra here on the Spanish *Camino* that France is too expensive and the French too rude. Lalalalaa.

That same Vancouver Donald and his daughter thought there were no English guidebooks so they walked the *Camino del Norte* by painstakingly translating a blog written in Catalan. I showed them an English guide from the Confraternity of St. James I have been using. I showed them the Fraternity's list of publications includes the *del Norte*. Later, I heard them telling their same story to another pilgrim—there was nothing in English so they translated from the Catalan. Reality does not fit their story. Lalalalaa.

And this is what I realized. We bring our stories. We bring our quests. We bring ourselves. We don't get to borrow another self for the walk. We bring who we are. We learn along the way. We leave behind extra baggage, but we never leave behind ourselves. I learned much from this walk and I had many beautiful experiences but it was always me doing the walking. My plan and me.

I am pondering the role of my own plan. I had a goal—to walk from Arles to Puente la Reina. I would not have come to Europe and slung on a backpack without that goal. I would not have kept walking in the rain if I had just said I think I will go meander around France. In addition to the destination, I had a quest. I had a reason to pay attention to what I saw and what I was learning. To be ever in the moment of walking, of moving forward, of observing and being with not only my fellow pilgrims but also with the vultures and the butterflies. It was important to me to achieve my goal, to pursue my quest.

At one point I went back to the French Pyrenees because after all the rain and the winter snow, there was a moment of magic. I stayed only four days because I did not want to deviate too much from my stated objective of reaching Puente la Reina. I tried to book a return trip to the Pyrenees after I reach Puente la Reina but it will be high season and Bastille Day and that particular moment in time has passed. I must ask myself why I did not stay longer. But of course, I already know the answer, the me I brought with me, the goal-oriented me, could only deviate so much from my plan. How often have I let magic slip by while I was focused on getting to where I was going?

Very close to getting to where I was going,
Love,
Barbara

LETTER THIRTEEN

After Arriving
Puente La Reina
July 8

I have arrived! Puente la Reina, Navarro, Spain. Nine hundred kilometers, more or less. Destination reached. Goal achieved! Plan fulfilled!

Excuse me, I think I will sit down.

I spent my last night as a pilgrim a few kilometers outside of Puente la Reina in the town of Obanos. Most of the people I met in Spain are going on to Santiago but I will stop at my goal, which was always Puente la Reina. In the morning of my last day we walked into and through Puente la Reina, which presents a gauntlet of breakfast bars and souvenir shops. I said goodbye to my Spanish hiking mates where the bridge crosses the river. I turned back to find not a *refugio*, but a hotel. Having arrived, my pack suddenly felt weighty, my foot hurt, and I wanted nothing more than a shower and change of clothes.

Does one feel exalted when they complete their walk? Yes, of course, but also a bit sad. There is something wonderfully simple about rising every day and walking with friends to a new destination. Every day you know what your goal is and every day you accomplish that goal. Arriving means accomplishment but the simplicity of life on the trail comes to an end. I look in the hotel mirror and see that I should find a hairdresser to color my grey roots. I log into my emails to see what problems have accumulated at home. I notice that my favorite T-shirt is torn. All of this

happens so fast, on the same morning I arrive. Reality was patiently biding its time.

So I reached my destination but what about that other thing, that little theist quest thing I had going on?

I know this is the letter where I should write how I found God, or he found me, and how we talk every day and when we can't chat, we text or email, exchange photos of the family. We are best buds. I wish I could write that, but I cannot. So what does that make me if I did not walk away from this long walk a theist? Certainly not an atheist—they have much more certainty than I do. And agnostics always sound like they don't know and don't care—and I do care. I used to say pantheist but that is so wrong as I may not have walked away with a God-buddy but I did walk away with a sense of oneness and unity—that I am a small person taking up a small space in a very large and beautiful world.

- That the sheer beauty of it all leaves me in awe of nature, or I suppose more appropriately Nature.

- That the generosity and kindness of my fellow pilgrims leaves me in awe of other beings, or I suppose Beings.

- That our fragility and strength, that my fragility and strength, leaves me in awe of me, or I suppose Me.

- That even if I cannot chat up this oneness that I feel, I do walk away with a sense of oneness, or I suppose Oneness.

So I walk away from my walk knowing that I have learned from my journey. What I do not know, may never know, is if God was trying to talk to me but that the me I brought with me on this journey, just didn't (couldn't) hear. . . . Lalalalaa

Written Monday July 8 in Puente la Reina.

Tomorrow I leave for Pamplona and the festival of San Fermín and crazy people running from bulls in the street and getting drunk on Coca-Cola mixed with red wine (I do not know which is crazier, the run or the drink.).

Thank you all for coming on my journey with me.
It has been fun to share this walk with you,
Barbara

Epilogue

A Note from Pamploma

Epilogue
A Note from Pamploma

Tomorrow I leave for Barcelona (where I plan to see the Virgin of Montserrat, Barcelona's Black Madonna) and then on to Sitges. It seems I began this trip with Black Madonnas, bullfights, and birds and am ending the trip the same way.

Pamplona is beautiful. I would love to see it in a non-festival time when all the churches and museums are open. I will definitely come back. Here is a "sort of" summary of the festival.

1. Only about a dozen young men run fast enough to actually run in front of (or with) the bulls. Everyone else is just jumping out of the way and over the barriers . . . wisely enough. It is like the parting of the seas. Most people actually end up running behind the bulls. There was a huge argument when a man wanted to run with his nine-year old son and was told the boy was too young. I don't even want to know if he was an American but I fear so.

2. All the young people wearing white pants and shirts, red bandanas and red sashes around their waists are really good looking—except it turns out even youth looks pretty awful after staying up all night drinking. And the music and drinking does go all night—literally all night.

3. Old men, that would be men my age, with dreams of their youth show up, put on the white pants and shirts, red bandanas and then tie the red sashes under their beer guts. They strut about. It is not a good look—drunk or sober.

4. The bulls run to get to the bullring for the afternoon bullfights—so I went to one. It was—uh err—shocking. A neon sign introduces the picadores and matadores and the bull. The bull is introduced by number, name, skin color and weight (most are around 550 kilos and that is a lot of bull). There are brass bands all through the audience. The audience is singing and chanting—pretty much like a football game except no one does the wave. The music could not possibly be more inappropriate. They sang *Funiculi, Funicula* (Joy is everywhere, *Funiculi, Funicula*) just as the matador moved in for the kill. I was warned to sit under an overhang because beer is tossed down from the fans above over the fans below thoroughly soaking everyone. After the third kill, there is something like a seven inning stretch when everyone eats a sandwich. The matadors had a difficult time killing the bulls so there was a lot of slow bloody torture. The hotel owner explained to me that the crowd is so rowdy; the best matadors refuse to fight here. This explains the slow torture.

An odd aside is I spoke with some Americans who are here to run with the bulls. They claim to be totally and absolutely opposed to and abhor bullfights—never quite understanding why and where the bulls are running.

5. There are the same T-shirts here as we have in San Francisco, you know those white T-shirts with a red heart that say "I (heart) SF". This caught me off guard at first until I realized how flexible these shirts are. Here, they are "I love San Fermín" (this is after all the San Fermín Festival). Maybe in Santa Fe they are "I love Santa Fe", or maybe San Fernando.

6. I have no estimate but many restaurants and shops are owned by Chinese. They are the establishments that never close. I was told the Spanish government has made it easy for Chinese citizens to own businesses in hopes of creating more jobs for Spanish youth. The only problem, I have never seen anyone who wasn't Chinese working in these establishments. I have also been told and I guess I will see tomorrow that in Barcelona many of the paella restaurants are now owned and operated by Chinese people—I guess rice is rice.

7. After the first morning of watching the running of the bulls in person, I have stayed at my hotel and watched the event on TV with the hotel owner. Today was quite something. As I said before the bulls run in front of most of the runners but today something extraordinary happened. One of the bulls simply turned around and went after one of the young men running behind him. Despite all the efforts of the professionals to distract the bull and rescue the young man, the bull just kept bearing down on this one poor soul. Apparently bulls get fixated and are not easily distracted. Well, three people ended up in the hospital and it was frightening.

8. I highly recommend this festival if you like to be drunk in public, stay up all night partying, and shout a lot over loud music. Actually this festival was quite a surprise since mostly I had only heard about the running of the bulls and the drinking. What I found were six stages with all sorts of Basque music and dancing, interesting food tents for sampling regional specialties, and lots of sangria, which just makes you happy. It is a huge cultural exploration of Spain and I have enjoyed it thoroughly.

Home soon,
Barbara

HOME

Asking Friends

THE QUESTION

San Carlos, California
August 4

I ended this year's walk in Puente la Reina, Spain. Within two weeks my foot was better. Within three weeks I was home. The walk was finished but not the questions or the quest. An exchange of emails produced the following discussion and eventually a question about God to all of you.

I wrote to you:

"Hard to know exactly what difference it would make if I did believe in God. I wonder if I am not just jealous of my friends who do. I do not think I would be a better person. Some of the most prejudiced people I know claim a profound relationship with God and some of the kindest people are atheists. I do not like the idea of a God who helps one football team beat another or for that matter one warrior. So I am not looking for favors from an almighty. I certainly do not like all these religions that pit their God against your God and even ask you to kill in His name. So I do not want to be "right" or even part of a group that is more "right" than everyone else. I am older but I do not think I am looking for a little after-death security though I wouldn't mind it—let's face it the balance is weighted heavily on the life-already-lived versus life-left-to-live scale. I guess the main thing for me is it would make all this incredible beauty make sense and perhaps make it all more meaningful. A God would certainly help explain the wonder of butterfly wings. I guess what I do not know; would it make a difference in my waking everyday life? Would it?"

Thank you all for answering my question. The answers have been amazing. This is a small, rather unscientific survey since I asked only the fifty friends reading my letters from the *Chemin* and my friends tend to be kind and generous people (lucky me).

There is an equal distribution between believers and non-believers. There is no relationship between intelligence nurtured by scientific-education and belief. Some of the most intelligent, scientifically educated people I know are atheists. Some of the most intelligent, scientifically educated people I know have personal relationships with God. The atheists are as absolute in their beliefs as the believers (so perhaps believer is a misnomer).

Several believers wrote only to say that the question was too big and they could not begin to answer. Several of the disbelievers railed against—not God—but religions, or as I like to think of them, the God-clubs. I think that is too easy a target. A few years ago, I went to hear Christopher Hitchens speak about the non-existence of God. He also railed against religion.

On one of the rainy days when I was approaching the Pyrenees, I came upon a pigeon shooting *maison*. There was a large coup with huge pigeons that never flew and spent all their time eating. They looked like inflated basketballs with wings. There was a very long ladder that the hunters climbed to stand on a platform high above the coup. When the hunters were in place, these overfed, under-exercised birds were let out of their cage. Their attempted lift off looked more like balloons that had sprung a leak and were deflating in circles of exhaustion. The proud hunters raised their guns and shot them. And this is what I think Hitchens did with his argument by taking on the God clubs. He went for the fattest target. Many God clubs have gone pretty far off the rails including the one I love so much, Catholicism. I imagine if God has feet, even He (please forgive the he but I get tired of managing the (s)he/it writing style), I imagine that even He feels sometimes like the God clubs are something he stepped in and would like to wipe off His shoes.

There is no relationship between "goodness" and belief. One of the most abusive and bigoted people I know has a warm and active relationship with God. He is a microcosm of everything that explodes in the off-the-rails god clubs. His relationship with god supports his self-righteous belief that he owns the truth and is superior and that God has chosen to speak to him. He and God chat frequently but apparently never about equality or justice.

On the other hand, one of the staunchest atheists lives an almost ascetic life because he feels responsible for the earth and other beings. Non-believers felt there was no God to fall back on, no after life to make up for this life, and that this world, our world, was our responsibility. There was no one who would forgive them if they acted selfishly. They felt actively responsible and are living lives reflective of that sense of responsibility.

One friend wrote:

"NOT believing in God . . . (and by that I mean a "personal" God who cares about me and human affairs)

1. Frees me from wondering why s/he/it would allow such horrible things to happen in the world

2. Brings me closer to other human beings, since it up to "us" to help each other and build a better world

3. Pushes me to focus on the here and now since I cannot rely on an after-life (which is generally associated with a belief in God)

4. Pushes me to give my life a meaning that is independent of God's "will"

5. Allows me to be in awe of the universe and accept my complete lack of understanding of its existence without the very limiting and naive notions we normally attach to the idea of God."

In fact, very few believers said they would live differently if there were no God. They are not motivated to do good by fear of God's retribution or reward, but by the same feeling of responsibility as the non-believers. There was a universal sense that we should make our lives and the lives of those around us happy and fulfilled. It made me wonder if people establish their moral compass and then, backfill their beliefs to support the magnetic pull of that compass.

One friend wrote, "I sometimes think we are better off not knowing. We are then left to develop our own moral guidelines. We are free to connect with the "G-d within", whatever that is. For me it is that part of me with the highest ideals. The part that truly cares about everyone and everything. Sadly, I fall so very short of my ideals."

Another friend wrote, "But still, a belief in God biases my interpretations to a universe that is evolving toward good (opportunity for full expression, equality, peace, creativity) rather than just chaotically. Religions based on rewards or punishments in the afterlife are like a set of training wheels for humanity as we learn to base our decisions on the true, long term best interests of our species and environment."

With only a few exceptions, believers had no God club and those with a God club had open eyes as to the advantages and faults of that club. No one in this particular group was enchanted by the club alone. No one responded with descriptions of a glorious afterlife. No one responded with the power of being right or part of a club that was always superior, always right, the owners of all truth. No believers felt obliged to proselytize for their club. Oddly, several non-believers proselytized heavily to *not* believe. In fact, non-believers were much more insistent than believers.

Believers wrote about the comfort of having an explanation for the sheer magnitude and beauty of the universe. A friend woke in the middle of the night thinking of my question and he thought, "hail fellow well met!" One opens the door in the morning and exalts in the amazing beauty of the world. That God must indeed be a very amiable and accomplished fellow! There was a spark of genius that began it all. But is it enough to say that God was one hell of a great designer and architect? Like so many other Silicon Valley entrepreneurs, he kicked off a great experiment and then retired from the scene? Where's the everyday plan, the Google calendar? Where's the day-to-day?

Many believers wrote about something I had not thought about. They wrote about unconditional love. About waking every day to the knowledge of being unconditionally loved. I understand unconditional love as something parents give their children. My father was sick and died long before I could know him and my mother only had one condition before she could give unconditional love, and her condition was to be a male not a female. I never had children to unconditionally love. Ah well. . . . So my understanding of this feeling is limited. Still . . . Am I seeking God because I am jealous of those of you who have this loving god in your lives? Who have this unconditional love? Maybe. . . . Another friend addresses this question differently, he says that believing in God makes it possible for him to love himself unconditionally. That is what the selfish me wants from a God.

Believers also wrote to say this was not a question one simply answered and put to bed like a tired child. No the child in this question wakes again and again in the night. It is a question to be visited and revisited. Just when you close your eyes and think you will get some rest the child wakes crying and the question must once again be answered. It's not easy having an existential child in the house.

Almost all the believers named God as Love, an essence internal or external or both—an essence so profound it changes everything about the way we view life. I finally realized all those who wrote to me about their life with God were trying to explain the unexplainable. It was like asking someone what is it like to be in love? You know when you feel it and all the poets in the world cannot explain it to one who has never felt it.

As many of you know I only have one good eye and have never seen binocular depth perception. I can only guess at what it is you see. I know you have a lot better shot at hitting the tennis ball than I do and that I was the worst outfielder who ever stood in left field. When I had my art show in Italy, one of the critics raved about my cleverness in jumbling the background into the foreground. Uh, not that clever. It is just the way I see the world. It is all that I have ever seen. If we go together to a magic show I will think you are an idiot because every time the girl with the long blonde hair sitting on the white horse magically disappears and you ooh and ah, I see the trick, not the magic. Because I have no binocular vision, I cannot see an optical illusion. You can explain what you see to me, but I can only sort of imagine it. I think I know what you mean, but of course, I do not. I understand when you watched the movie *Avatar*, motions fairly popped off the screen. I saw a movie that looked pretty much like the word I see. Flat. I wish I could see what you see but my brain has never connected my left eye to my right eye. I have accepted the fact that it never will.

I am less content to accept this lack of understanding about God. Most of you wrote that believing in God starts with believing in the possibility of God. There is no other place to begin. So I will continue to seek and to wonder and perhaps out of jealousy and perhaps because I still need a better explanation of the beauty of butterfly wings. I want to know if when one sees the silhouette of a saguaro against the desert sunset if maybe one should say bravo or brava or bravi . . . hail fellow, well met, well done, well done indeed!

Sent August 4 from San Carlos, CA

Love. Barbara

The Answers

San Carlos, California
August 2013

I will respond as I have been responding for years to this issue—If I am to accept the existence of God, I feel that the burden of proof is on him, not me. So far, I am unconvinced. And frankly, if there is a God, He has a hell of a lot to answer for.

Heretically, your friend

I'd love to give my answer to your question! It makes all the difference of the world to believe in God. You'll know it when you have found God in yourself and in all that lives. God is eternal now, eternal love, eternal life. With this belief, or better, knowledge, you know that you are always loved. That's the difference. If you don't believe in God you need confirmation that you are ok from outside yourself, if you believe in God you know that you are ok, even if you make mistakes.

I don't believe in God. But I think that for people who do believe in God, it makes a big difference. They think about God a lot, and they change their behavior because of their beliefs about God. I don't, and that's pretty different.

On NPR the other day I heard a guy being interviewed about Muslim finance laws. Apparently you're not supposed to earn or pay interest if you're a Muslim. At one point in the interview this guy said, "It's the first thing I think about when I wake up, and the last thing I think about a night before I go to sleep." I'd say that for him, believing in God makes a big difference!

I could write a dissertation on this one. It makes a big difference: self-determination, self-responsibility, self and social accountability, etc. But think of all the great art that has resulted from the belief!

I think it makes a difference if you say one thing but believe another. I tried to believe in god, and just couldn't do it, and felt like a liar saying I did. I would assume the same would go for someone like my wife, who is absolutely rational and science-based, yet cannot shake her profound faith in the God of the Catholic church (even though she totally disavows any alliance with the Vatican). We even tried going to an Episcopal church as a sort of compromise, and she really dug it, but it wasn't her church.

A quick response from me: I do believe in God, and am rather active in a socially progressive Christian denomination (United Church of Christ) church in Palo Alto. For me the community of worship and fellowship, support and music/meditation is all an important part of my life, but is mostly significant for the social and justice aspects that don't strictly require a theology. But still, a belief in God biases my interpretations to a universe that is evolving toward good (opportunity for full expression, equality, peace, creativity) rather than just chaotically. Religions based on rewards or punishments in the afterlife are like a set of training wheels for humanity as we learn to base our decisions on the true, long term best interests of our species and environment.

NOT believing in god . . . (and by that I mean a "personal" god who cares about me and human affairs)

1. Frees me from wondering why s/he/it would allow such horrible things to happen in the world

2. Brings me closer to other human beings, since it up to "us" to help each other and build a better world

3. Pushes me to focus on the here and now since I cannot rely on an after-life (which is generally associated with a belief in god)

4. Pushes me to give my life a meaning that is independent of god's "will"

5. Allows me to be in awe of the universe and accept my complete lack of understanding of its existence without the very limiting and naive notions we normally attach to the idea of god

I should say that believing in a god is not a choice. I don't know how anyone can choose to believe something or not. You believe based on the evidence before you.

Regardless, I think that it makes a difference if you think that you know what this god wants you to do (based on written documents or some telepathic means) and you take actions according to this belief. In other words, it makes a difference if you do not use your own intellect and take personal responsibility for your life decisions.

I hope this helps: I don't believe in god. I don't subscribe to the Enlightenment era fantasy that everything in the universe can be understood and explained by the science of man but I also don't connect to religious doctrine, Jewish, Christian, Buddhist, or otherwise.

In the middle of the night words came to me: "Hail fellow well met." It's not an expression I ever use. Don't remember ever using it at all. I knew it had something to do with your question and it woke me up. Clearly divine inspiration. It's appropriate, don't you think? If we're talking about eternity, wouldn't we want someone with an amiable personality to spend it with? So much of creation is breathtakingly beautiful. Don't you open your front door sometimes and step out, look around, and say: "Well done old chap. Good job." An amiable fellow must have done all that. But it's not always so. Sometimes the view is not so agreeable. I'm in a very cheerful mood at the moment and don't want to think of the other views, but other words come to mind. "By his works ye shall know him." "What hath God wrought?" I know your question was about whether the fellow, amiable or otherwise exists at all, but my mind keeps working at the other end. Can't we get some clue about this hypothetical creator by looking at what he presumably created? I really don't have an answer to your question.

However, I will state my belief to you. I have never believed that a god could exist to create and destroy this universe.

I am not a fanatic who argues against the beliefs of others. I am more of the "whatever floats your boat" philosophy. I guess that puts me in the "doesn't make a difference" clan. However, we know that religious zealots can alienate all others to promote their agenda. I don't know that Atheist or Agnostics have ever purged the population to advance their agenda.

Don't know who else asked U, but since I asked, here's another query: which god or goddess R U thinking of? There R Hindu, Buddhist, Jewish, Protestant, as well as Egyptian, Roman, Greek, etc. Can U pin it, him/her/them down a little?

Small question.

One could speculate that a belief in god(s) or God (if you think you got the right one) is the product of mystified people trying to comprehend things they didn't understand, that such belief somehow summed it all up in a way that explained life giving meaning to existence, and eventually offered something beyond life's obvious limitations. It also offered a social order that with enough community buy-in helped build civic commons and make an otherwise dangerous the world a little safer.

One might think that except for the self-preservation imperative of religious institutions imposing belief on the least educated of humanity, religious thinking would have long ago disappeared; replaced by reasoned scientific explanations, common sense, and intuitive explanation. But that did not happen. While religious institutions appear ever more insane in their conservation of the past, the spiritual impulse itself continues to revive in new contexts wanting to give meaning to our human experience.

Even the most advanced cultures recognize the limitations of human knowledge. Whereas one context of understanding may have informed the life of someone living in the Dark Ages, new contexts of understanding now form like an endless series of waves washing ashore with increasing rapidity. One might be impressed by the accumulation of knowledge and meaning, but must also be constantly reminded as to how much is not known—not just what we know we don't know but what we don't know that we don't know and is only a faint glimmer on the far distance. We are peeling an onion from the inside out and regardless of how crystallized our understanding of the current layer, for anyone looking beyond (not trying to draw small comfort by adopting a fixed position) the layers seem infinite.

While the hierarchical institutions with their brokered interpreted meaning may be gone from our consciousness, in facing the ever present unknown there is still an unknowable that commands our presence, contemplation and respect. Call it what you like; god is as good a term as any (there's tradition there), our capacity to experience the rapt awe of that which is beyond our capacity to fully process is one of things that most informs that life is worth living. After all, how many times do people say "Oh my god" while having sex—I rest my case.

. . . .

I cannot imagine a universe that does not have a creator. For me, not having a sense of the transcendent meaning of the totality of existence would remove the awe, mystery and reverence I feel every day. Quarks and string theory are just not enough.

. . . .

We already touched your question when you passed last year in Auvillar. Your questions are stimulating and never easy. Thank you.

To answer to this question my English is to poor and you must content you with my language level. But questions and answers (dialogue) are the onliest way to find the truth even with a bad English. Here my answer:

We do not know who or what is God. This is surmounting our sensual and rational facilities. We only can approach to him in belief. We can only believe in him or not believe. In this point of view it does not make a difference to believe or not believe in a God. Believing and not believing is the same effort every time.

But to believe (or not believe) without reason, mind and heart is not appropriate for us as adult beings of the present age with its level of science and culture. And your question is excluding an indifferent relationship to God: God cannot make any difference to a normally cultured modern man. Once more: We only can believe in him or not believe in him and always with effort and labor. He is a constant existential challenge.

But your question is personal (as all your questions). You want to know, if it makes a difference for me. After more than seven decades way of life, I must say that it makes a big difference. Not to believe in God would be for me a loss of quality of life. Life would not have sense for me. I would have a shortened and poorer access to the true, good and beautiful, to those categories of the reality, which I only can approximate and never can grasp totally, similar my approach to God. That means on the other side that I do not need God as a severe judge, as someone who is responsible for our calamities and crimes. In my belief she/he is love and merits an adequate approach.

. . . .

As you might expect, I have pondered this quite a bit over the years. I like to revisit this question periodically to see if getting older and mellowing changes things.

My position has remained the same for me. Since my values drive my behavior and I do not take any actions based on any ultimate prospect of a "payoff" (heaven), nor driven by fear of ultimate suffering (hell), I would do the same things whether there is a G-d or not. Therefore, it doesn't matter in terms of effecting my actions.

However, as I am getting older and somewhat less weighted down by heavy decisions with potentially far ranging consequences, I often find myself pondering whether there is meaning and purpose to life. Is life heading somewhere and each of us has a responsibility to contribute to the progress of the universe? Is life just an accident and going nowhere and therefore nothing matters on the grand scale at all? Do we infuse life with meaning by our values and principles?

Well, even if there is no intelligent design and purpose to life, we still have the opportunity to make it the best life possible for ourselves and for the rest of all those who find themselves existing side by side with us. So again, does it really matter beyond curiosity and wanting to know everything there is to know?

I sometimes think we are better off not knowing. We are then left to develop our own moral guidelines. We are free to connect with the "G-d within", whatever that is. For me it is that part of me with the highest ideals. The part that truly cares about everyone and everything. Sadly, I fall so very short of my ideals. Against that yardstick I feel myself having fallen short in so many ways . . . of not having fully taken advantage of the gifts I have been given and , sadly, I have failed to fulfill my potential.

I wonder about that "G-d within". Where does it come from? If there is a G-d and we are made in its image then that is the connection. Is that connection a real time communication to something outside ourselves? Or does it reside completely with us, independent of everything else?

In the end, for me, it is about connecting to, honoring and allowing myself to be guided by "it". That for me is spirituality and doesn't require a belief in a personified G-d or any formal religion . . . not that I have anything against either if that's what works for some people. I do believe that you can't let someone else tell you what G-d wants, as if G-d talks only to them and you are too lowly to ever know for yourself.

So, is there a G-d? When it helps me in some way to accept that possibility, I do. But at other times I find it more important to accept personal responsibility and not use G-d as an excuse to let myself off the hook; at those time I comfort myself with the possibility that there may be no G-d and it is up to each us to co-create life as we wish to know.

. . . .

It is indeed a very interesting question and also the entrance to a rabbit hole that will go about as deep as you dare to go. But given that I happen to have a moment of time on my hands and love rollercoasters I'll give it a plunge with you if you care to follow.

In order to approach this question I would first take a step back to look at what reality is. There has been one person in the world I know of that has come closest to understand that mystery and that person was Helen Keller.

I'll assume we all know the story so I'll get right to it: She described herself before she got language in her own words as "an unconscious clod of earth". Unconscious is the key word here, without language there was no consciousness present in her. Life maybe, and reactions to her environment, but no consciousness. No concept of self, of pain, joy, or any emotion, merely reaction to stimulus.

When language finally entered her world in that one moment when the sensation of water on her skin miraculously connected with her caretaker spelling w a t e r in her hand consciousness arose in her. An entire universe was born. She later said: "That living word awakened my soul, gave it light, hope, joy, set it free".

Now I wouldn't necessarily quite go as far out as to say that without language there is no soul but there certainly is no consciousness without it.

Funny enough the Bible also says: "In the beginning was the Word, and the Word was with God, and the Word was God." And you'll find similar hints in just about any religion.

The word creates, language is creation.

And now comes the fun part. Based on this all of what we know as creation arises in language because our consciousness itself is language. We are the ones creating the world through god, including god itself. If you're uncomfortable with that, you could also say god creates the world through the word of our consciousness including him (or her)self. But it is the same thing because the speaking happens with us, in our consciousness. Language is the soul of humanity; it is the soul of creation.

Now how come humanity has language is a whole other tunnel I won't go down at this juncture but my point is that the word found Helen Keller and she from it created a world including the words.

So to your question does it make a difference to believe in god or even gods as the case may be?

Well the answer to that is in what you yourself say. And I mean as in literally what you say. Your word creates your reality whether you are aware of it or not.

The most tragically funny thing about us as human beings is that we by default think our words describe reality when they in fact create it!

Ever wondered how come that there is millions of Christians for example who all say they believe in (the) one God but have over the course of history done any range of things in his name from the most gracious acts of compassion to the most atrocious deeds? If you compare what being a true Christian is in the eyes of different churches or even for different groups within one church it makes you wonder if they seriously can all be talking about the same thing.

And that's because they're not. Every person creates a different god, i.e. has perforce a different "understanding" of god and acts accordingly.

It was mostly "the good people" who burned witches out of fear of damnation and the devil. We all do what we think is "right" and act upon how the world occurs to us without even realizing that we make up all the meaning in our world through our point of view (and then often suffer from it). If there is one thing in existence that truly is ours then it is our word; we do have a say.

Some people find solace, love, and peace in their belief in god while others live a life of terror, trying to ask for forgiveness from an unforgiving god they believe in. Again others reject the whole thing altogether as silly and prefer not to think about it, all the while still creating (they would probably say "describing" or "understanding") the world they live in. It's just that the majority never realized they had a say and just took over what they were told by others for better or worse.

As for me—I realized that I prefer to live in wonder. I believe butterflies are not insects but messengers from another realm. Why? Because I like that and it adds mystery to my life. I don't care if I'm not "right" in the current eyes of science. My point of view about butterflies is not threatened by other people's points of view. I also believe in all kinds of gods because—heck why not? If there was just one he'd grow bored.

I have little altars for my gods and every now and then I bring them a little gift because everybody likes gifts. And if something happens that I like then I believe it's a gift from them. Sometimes they're being grumpy and challenge me, sometimes I'm grumpy and challenge them. I made them in my likeness and I am made after them.

I am dead serious about this and I also make it all up at the same time and laugh. Or maybe the gods all make themselves up through me and I occasionally doubt that, who is to say. That's why it's called belief. My rule of thumb regarding gods is if they can't handle that I laugh about them from time to time they're not fit to be my gods and vice versa.

I'm creating my belief and I am doing the believing as a matter of honoring my word (i. e. god) and it works for me which is why I do it.

But if you're up for an experiment try this: the next time you come to a rose bush sit down in front of it. Take a moment to look at its blossoms and smell them, then say a little prayer to it. Anything, whatever is on your mind, if you don't know what to say just flatter it, flowers love that. But they are extremely good at listening. They will, however, hear you best if you whisper directly into their blossoms.

And who knows you just may end up talking to god. Or not.

It is up to you.

. . . .

(reply to above)

Thank you for your email, I'm a friend of Barbara's, and your email got me thinking. I wanted to make sure that I understand your logic and point of view, so the purpose of this email is to clarify what you are saying. Let's see if I "got it"

We know that if an accident happens on the corner of an intersection, and we interview five witnesses, we'll get five different stories of what happened with contradictory information. For each of them, their perception of the event is equivalent to the reality of the event. What they saw is their view of reality. Ask a husband and wife about how they met and you'll get different versions too. "She was wearing a blue dress" and "I was wearing a green dress." How we each see the world is very different. I imagine that if a prosecutor interviewed four witnesses and they all said exactly the same thing, then the prosecutor would firmly believe that they were colluding. So we know that we see the world differently through our unique lenses.

Our unique perspectives on reality would partially explain why we have different views of god, ethics, and religion. Yet, I think you are going one step further. I think you are saying that these perceptions become reality for each of us. That for each of us, our perception of god really becomes god. Then, let me try to apply this logic to another case to see if I understand your point of view. I'll choose the President of the United States. A large group of people think he is a fantastic president. A large group of people think he is a horrible president. While we all elected someone to be President, each of us views his actions and beliefs differently. For the lovers, in their mind's eye, there really is a person who can do no wrong. For the haters, in their mind's eye, there really is a person who can do no right. So, in reality, there are really multiple presidents. There's at least three, and less than eight billion. Perhaps each person who has heard of him, has their own version of him. Maybe people who have never heard of him, since they don't know who he is, don't have a copy. So maybe there are a billion or so Presidents of the United States in existence. When we think about god, we each create a god.

You also mentioned that god creates us. So as I wander through my day, the people I meet are also creating me. Clearly they are affecting me: people will say yes, say no, smile, frown, open a door, close a door, etc., but are their perceptions of me altering me, or do we each have a copy of me?

You can tell from my email where I'm coming from. As I type this email, I think of myself as one person, much as I would think the President of the United States thinks of himself as one person. Yet everyone who I meet today, really believes in a different me. In short, reality is really in our heads, not outside ourselves.

Am I close?

. . . .

Whew—what a question to try to answer in an email! First, let me give you the name of some books that were helpful to a friend who had a similar question. They were written by people that were much better communicators and thinkers than I am!

The Language of God, Francis S. Collins (Free Press, 2006)

The Reason for God, Timothy Keller (Dutton, 2007)

Simply Christian, N.T. Wright (HarperOne, 2010)

Secondly, as to my thoughts, I suppose you won't be surprised when I tell you that I simply cannot imagine going through the complexities that life presents without having faith and trust in God, who I believe to be the creator of all things. For me to know that God loves me despite myself, that He understands and forgives me, and that He made me because He wants to be in constant conversation with me, allows me to be at peace with my place in the world despite what my surroundings communicate to me. Further, believing God "has the whole world in His hands" and that His plan, His desire, is the very best for us, gives me peace in the midst of many troubled times and in the midst of many troubling questions that come up in life, even though it doesn't always look pretty in the short term of life on Earth. So then why do bad things happen to good people? That's a whole different discussion. But hearing our preacher's answer to my Bible Studies group, it makes sense and so while still difficult, I "get it" as much as mankind can ever get it.

Why do I so confidently have that belief, peace and trust that makes such a difference in my life? It's been an interesting thing for me to have studied the Old Testament as I have for our little Bible Study. I've seen that from the time of Adam and Eve's big mistake in the garden, God has been looking for man to communicate with him about the things that they did wrong so that He could show them His love by forgiving them. His ultimate expression of that is, of course, having sent His Son Jesus so that He could die on the cross for the ultimate expression of God's forgiveness and love for us. Jesus' appearance to so many after His resurrection shows us that God gives us hope of a wonderful life after our physical death here, and that if God can conquer death and Satan, then think of all that He can do for us today and into eternity. (As hard as Jesus' resurrection is to believe, his resurrection appearances is what caused belief in Him to grow and continue until today. Interestingly, despite the Apostles spending three years with Him before

His death, they never really understood the He was God's son and the promised Messiah until after His resurrection appearances. After that, they got it to the point that most all Apostles suffered terrible deaths because of their belief in Him.)

To add a deeper level and perhaps complexity, Jesus is believed by Christians to be God that came to Earth to show us what true love really is. I am sure you know all of this, so forgive me, but. . . . In the Old Testament God told people how to behave, and as any parent would He disciplined them gently and progressively more strongly, until they got the picture. As they kept falling away from truly loving one another (i.e. laws like the 10 Commandments), He came to Earth Himself in the form of Jesus to show us what words couldn't adequately demonstrate. True love, how to treat one another, and ultimately His unconditional love and forgiveness through his death on the cross for those who live apart from the will of God for their lives, which of course is all of us in varying degrees. The symbolism of the final, sacrificial unblemished lamb to redeem people from their sinful ways, could not have been missed by devout Jews who had practiced this since the days of Abraham.

So, then what about all of the terrible things people do in the name of Religion and/or Christianity . . . what about when they (these people) take matters into their own hands and don't follow the rules set out by Jesus? They simply aren't following Jesus' example and commands. Jesus never tried to raise an army and never told anyone to fight. He simply loved people into loving Him—by understanding and forgiving, and by letting them decide for themselves . . . as Christians should do more of today if they really want to follow Him.

As to your friend's question about which god based upon which religion are you speaking of? Jesus came proclaiming He was God. All other leaders of other faiths came proclaiming to speak for God. I have read the book *Religions of Man* by Huston Smith (Joanna Cotler Books, 1965) several times as I tried to understand the different religions. I found it was pretty good at separating them out, at least for me.

It's been long enough since I've read all of your wonderful trip notes that I don't remember all of your thoughts, but I do remember you saying that you tried speaking to God, but that you supposed He didn't want to talk to you! Well, I think that your desire to speak to Him is actually a result of Him "speaking" to you—in your heart and your mind. It's just pretty tough since we don't get an audible voice, but as I tell many friends, conversations with God are like conversations with friends—if you do all of the talking you never get a chance to hear what THEY have to say. And if you really want to know them, you'll be quiet a while and let them talk. And if you REALLY want to get to know them, then you will even read what they wrote. So to me, and for Christians, reading what God wrote to us is of course the Bible. Is it difficult to read? Of course it can be. But with a good modern day translation, and a focus on the right books in the Bible, it's quite wonderful and certainly helpful! Also know that I believe God speaks to us through the words and actions of others.

So has God spoken to you? I believe He in fact has. Initially and continually, through that restless and relentless question and desire for a conversation, a relationship, with Him. You, I know, have heard, "Our hearts are restless until they rest in Him." That is because the Old Testament tells us that all of creation was made because of God's loneliness. He wants a relationship with you, and all of mankind, because He made mankind for himself.

When you realize that through the years man has looked beyond what they saw and thought, hoped, believed, hoping that there was a higher power, I believe it was God seeking them by causing them to seek Him. I believe the majesty of nature, the beauty of butterfly wings, the complexity of all that exists in the universe, calls us to Him. I believe that those today who turn from that relentless call of God (to Buddha, or adamantly away from God) do so in part because of the terrible things that Christians have done, said, expected of others, in the name of God; the terribly non-Christian ways and words of well-intentioned Christians that turn people away from God, rather than towards Him.

So, there is my little answer to your little question. I'm sure it's not complete at answering the questions in your mind, and it sure isn't complete at discussing all of the complexities of God, religion, and life, but it's my starter thoughts. And all of this is why I believe God is important to me in the living of my life. I'd love to talk to you about it sometime if you'd like. And I'd love to hear your thoughts as well!

Until then, whenever I see butterflies I'll think of you and see them as angel wings—which they could very well be.

· ·

Getting back to your original question about would "believing in god change your life," I think it really depends upon your definition of "believe" and your definition of "god"—I have several friends who believe that the doorknob is god or that a group of people in a room, the collective consciousness is god. For them, I don't think "believing in god" really does change their lives, I mean, how could it? Most of my friends who fall into this camp really struggle with the concept of god due to childhood or young adult issues. Their stories are really sad, and I applaud them for trying.

I mentioned Jesus, because of our mutual backgrounds. If he really is god as he claims to be, then it might be worth reading what he says about talking with god. I've been re-reading Bible stories in "the message" translation and they have been very impactful. There is no way that Hollywood would ever accept "David and Goliath" as a movie script, it reads like a movie targeted for kids. So the President of the United States allows this boy to represent the country in fierce battle because none of the GI Joes are brave enough? We already have *Spy Kids 3*. Next script please!

I need to write more about my own story and my own struggle about "worth"—while I intellectually know that I have worth, my core inner being does not believe this to be true. I've grown up with the lie that I have no value (which explains why I like to excel at work and earn my own worth.) I'm stuck. I've wanted out. I've been actively working on this for several months, and no progress. When asked, "Are there any reasons why I shouldn't be worthy", I am able to honestly say no. Thus I know that it is something that I'm holding on to. I loved your post about Lalalalalalala. That's what I'm doing. All this truth says that God loves me incredibly so, yet I'm actively resisting that love. Arrrrrg. Several people have suggested that I read Psalm 139. Have I done that? No! Lalalalalala I mentioned your story to a close friend and he suggested Psalm 139 for you. Have I still read it? No! Lalallaalalla I want and don't want to believe it. So I'll schedule time to read it before my next email.

God, investigate my life;
get all the facts firsthand.
I'm an open book to you;
even from a distance, you know what I'm thinking.
You know when I leave and when I get back;
I'm never out of your sight.
You know everything I'm going to say
before I start the first sentence.
I look behind me and you're there,
then up ahead and you're there, too—
your reassuring presence, coming and going.
This is too much, too wonderful—
I can't take it all in!

ACKNOWLEDGMENTS

Thank you to Alberto Cabrera Aguiar, Marie-Claude, Maite Ozkoidi, Amadeu and Escarlate Senabre, Peter and Suzanne Van Vilet, Lou, Andy and Sam Asman, and all the other pilgrims who walked with me on these journeys. Thank you to all the friends and family who allowed me to print your responses to my query about God. A special thank-you to Marie-Claude, Alberto Cabrera Aguiar, Maite Ozkoidi, and Suzanne and Peter Van Vilet for providing me with your lovely photographs. Thank you to Incanto Press (Peter Miller, Kendall Kaufmann, Irina Yuzhakova, Joanne Naiman, Kate Davidson) for asking to publish my letters and working so hard to make this book a reality.

COMMUNITY

Join the community of readers discussing *Letters from The Way*. Scan the QR code below with your smartphone.

Conditions of the Delivery of the "Creanciale"

The "creanciale" is delivered by a religious leader or a delegate of the Catholic Church. Its delivery does not require being Christian, but perhaps the opportunity of a fraternal and trusting dialogue opening up a spiritual deepening of the pilgrimage. This document cannot be given through the mail; it is given by hand. The "creanciale" is then the sign of a confident and reciprocated welcome between the pilgrim and the church.

The "creanciale" can accompany this informative guide.

The priests, deacons, religious and community leaders can get their "creanciale" and their guide from:

Diocesan secretariat of pilgrimages

1 rue Frayssinous – BP 821 – Diocese of Rodez

Diocesan directors of pilgrimages

Practical Information

Traditionally the pilgrimage is done on foot and in a single go. For guidance, the marked trail of Puy at Saint-Jacques asks for about two months, on foot, to cover 1600 km (994 miles). Today, the church gives the "compostela" (attestation of the pilgrimage) in the entry of the Saint-Jacques cathedral, given the "creanciale" properly buffered daily (it is asked to have done at least the last 100 kilometers by foot or 200 by bike or other non-motorized way)

Whatever the chosen itinerary (topographic guides exist), it is suggested to get equipped "lightly" (bag under 12 kg) and to start out slowly. It is deeply recommended to take advice from former pilgrims. In all French regions, jacquaires associations allow for meetings and provide all useful information (equipment, itineraries, budget, books . . .).